Hypnotical deprogramming addiction!

Strategic confessions of a Rogue Hypnotist!

By the Rogue Hypnotist.

A convention of British English punctuation and spelling is used throughout. I have used an older convention of placing apostrophes after dates, e.g. 1500's. This is a stylistic preference. Script formats (though no content!) have been compressed from the kindle version to save you lots of money.

<u>Also in this internationally bestselling series...</u>

- ***How to Hypnotise Anyone - Confessions of a Rogue Hypnotist.***
- ***Mastering Hypnotic Language - Further Confessions of a Rogue Hypnotist.***
- ***Powerful Hypnosis - Revealing Confessions of a Rogue Hypnotist.***
- ***Forbidden hypnotic secrets! - Incredible confessions of the Rogue Hypnotist.***
- ***Wizards of trance - Influential confessions of a Rogue Hypnotist.***
- ***Crafting hypnotic spells! - Casebook confessions of a Rogue Hypnotist.***

<u>Coming soon –</u>

- ***Hypnotically annihilating anxiety - Penetrating confessions of a Rogue Hypnotist.***

And the final Rogue Hypnotist book...

CONTENTS

Acknowledgements

Dedicated to my failures, which taught me how to succeed.

Drugs hurt the mind, have power to cause madness.'

Ovid, 'The Art of Love.'

Introduction: why read this book?

BOOK 8 in the Rogue Hypnotist series is here! Although part of a series, this book stands alone too!

THIS BOOK WILL SAVE YOU 1000s of $s and £s in training courses and books! I planned it that way! It is quick, easy and to the point! **I believe that although this book is not 1000% comprehensive, it will arm you with the most powerful and most-comprehensive kit of addiction beating hypnosis scripts out there!**

Addiction is everywhere! It is a modern, socially acceptable plague. Humans are highly prone to 'addiction' or what we call addiction for convenience sake. Addictions to various things – drugs, TV, Internet, gambling, sex etc. all have the same root cause and because the cause is so commonplace we are going to have problems with addiction on planet earth for a long time to come. The cause of addiction is no mystery, it has nothing to do with your genes or any of that crap. Human misery is the cause of human addictive processes. But there is hope. A great deal of hope in fact.

This book is going to teach you how to 'CURE*' addictions – yes I did use to C word, no not the rude one, the C.U.R.E word. Now what do I mean by cure? I mean that you will guide a client through a process whereby they will 'self-cure'. We won't be faffing around with 'treatments' – this book will give you at a very lost cost the not so secret keys to 'cure' a whole host of addictions using the hypnotic deprogramming blueprints I will clearly and easily lay out in this book. Too many people are suffering, their families are suffering, society is suffering – if this book helps one health practitioner cure just one person of their addiction the Rogue Hypnotist will be a happy hypnotist indeed. Like my 6th book 'Crafting hypnotic spells', this book is a script fest. Technique junkies will be happy!

(*I have to keep using quotes around the word 'cure' for legal reasons.)

I have written 7 internationally bestselling books on Amazon. This was entirely by accident; no one was more shocked and humbled than me! I am a highly successful qualified professional hypnotherapist and Master Practitioner of NLP (sounds grander than it is!) working in London, England. I can cure 99.9% of my clients in one, one hour session for a vast number of problems – curing anxiety disorders is one of my specialities; the actual processes I use to do so will be fully outlined in my next book. The other field, if you can call it that, is addiction. I have cured more people of addictions than most people have had hot dinners – the secret is: it's easy IF the client wants to change. If the client wants you the therapist to *do the work* – they're in big trouble with a capital F for f**ked! This is a no nonsense practical book. I am ready to spill the beans – are you ready to severely kick addiction's sweaty ass!?

The good thing is there are multiple way to do the job...in many ways this book and its immediate soon to be published successor on anxiety are advanced complementary volumes to book 3, 'Powerful hypnosis' in which I broadly speaking outlined my highly successful approach to therapy. You are now going to get specifics.

Like my other ones, this book is not dry, academic and dull; it uses humour, irony, cheekiness, fun and a certain irreverence to teach you. I remain an anonymous hypnotist. I learned how to do this with clients who are all normal, everyday folk like you and me: not seedy rock and roll drug fiends, not amoral junkies of the worst kind: just ordinary men and women who were suffering. Let's do it!!!

The nature of humans, the nature of addictions.

There is little theory in your book because addiction is simple and straightforward, no matter what crud you may have learnt to the contrary. If you have read my other books you'll know I like to play with word origins to at least try to find out the real meaning of words. Let's take...

Addiction (Note: those of you into psycho and neuro-lingusitics – the word 'addiction' is a nominalisation). From 1600's sense of 'tendency', of **habits, pursuits**, etc. From 1640's as 'state of being self-addicted', derived from Latin 'addictionem' (nominative 'addictio') = 'an **awarding, a devoting**'. It was a noun of action from the past participle stem of 'addicere' (see 'addict' below). Interestingly the earliest recorded sense was less severe: '**inclination,** penchant'; this is now obsolete. The modern sense of addictions is recorded in 1906, in reference to opium (however, there is an isolated instance from 1779, with reference to tobacco).

In essence addiction is a pleasurable habit. At least, that's often how it starts. What about...

'Addict' (Note: this is an inaccurate static label that implies an identity level genetic basis to addiction – I have covered this in my other books.) First recorded in the 1530's (implied in 'addicted'); derived from Latin 'addictus', the past participle of 'addicere' - 'to deliver, **award, yield**; give assent, make over, **sell**', and figuratively, 'to devote, consecrate; **sacrifice, sell out, betray**'. From 'ad' – 'to' + 'dicere' = 'say, declare' (as in diction); but also, 'adjudge, allot'. In the 1520's the word meant – 'delivered, devoted'.

An 'addict', that is someone who is going through a temporary phase of the process we call 'addiction', is selling out their health, life and relationships at worst; they are abnormally focusing on the drug of no choice, whatever that may be.

Misery and addiction.

When people cannot get, or perceive that they cannot get their basic, fundamental universal human needs met, they are prone to develop addiction problems (see my other books and the section on missing need fulfilment in this book). That is when we are stressed, anxious and miserable we want a way out – a way to mask, to suppress the psychic and perhaps physical pain. We may turn to devices; external media etc. which can induce intense pleasure states in ways that so hypnotically absorb us that we forget about our troubles for a while. What starts out as a naughty 'treat' can turn into a prison.

Addiction is a coping habit: nothing more, nothing less. When we carry out the addiction patterns of behaviour long enough, the conscious act of using or taking the drug of no choice is taken over by the subconscious. You no longer have a choice about it – it has become wired in – looped as a pattern at the subconscious level. This is what produces the feeling of compulsion, impulse etc. It reality the act has become such a part of life that the subconscious, in response to certain inner and outer cues, performs the behaviour without conscious volition becoming involved. In effect the addictive process has become a post-hypnotic command.

Basically when we feel like crap for long enough we want to feel good – just for a while! We have indulged in a Gnostic fantasy: the idea that we can artificially induce pleasure and joy into our life, when what we need to do is fix our life or get a life first. ***In fact that is what cultural conditioning has disgracefully suggested to people in the modern world – the drive for pleasure funds a socially acceptable outlet in drugs!*** Guess what: incredibly happy and naturally satisfied people don't become addicts – it must be their genes. Balls! It must be their life.

As a therapist etc. you must teach your clients how to get satisfaction naturally. Later I'll show you just what to do.

Rogue Hypnotist's insight: addiction feels like hypnosis!

The fact is - the right **hypnotic interventions work with addictions because addictions are just like post-hypnotic commands! When a person with an addictive problem engages in the addictive act they are in a drug trance!** They are fixated and highly absorbed. In many ways you are waking them up from this 'drug-nosis' – snapping them out of it. I'll show you how. They key is *dissociation at the point of urge.* The scripts reveal all!!!

Cultural hypnosis and drugs – the 'It's okay to do drugs' culture.

Although personal factors such as a crap job, lack of money, loss of a loved one, overwork, bad or no close and intimate relationships, even lingering trauma may be linked to individual causes of addiction, the addiction explosion of the 20th century and the early 21st (it shows no signs of improving by the way) find their real roots in several ideological changes – 1. The emergence and dominance of secular humanistic philosophies that stress only the materialistic aspects of human existence – this produces a culture of hopeless nihilism – or 'winners and losers'. 2. The infiltration of Eastern Gnostic beliefs that reality is just a perception and that it can be transformed through taking actions that are fantastical and have no grounding in material fact. 3. The hedonistic culture of the 1960's – which produced the sexual, cultural and drug revolutions etc. In this period drug taking and promiscuity became 'normalised'. Pro-establishment drug promoters such as Dr. Timothy Leary (admitted C.I.A) and books like 'The Doors of Perception' by Aldous Huxley etc. did a great deal to 'psuedo-intellectualise' drug abuse amongst the 'educated' middle classes. 4. Globalisation, deindustrialisation and its permanent instability and change for changes sake: this causes massive social upheaval and a state of continual flux (see book 7 'Escaping cultural hypnosis'). 5. The New Age and so-called Human Potential Movements which promoted drug use as a way to achieve 'peak experiences' and transcend (trance-end) 'human limitations'; i.e. secular man as 'god' delusions. 6. The destruction of the nuclear and importantly *extended* family = smaller natural support networks. 7. Poverty. Being poor has not gone away – the gap between rich and poor is growing exponentially. The poor look to cheap drugs as they do to the fantasy of winning the lottery to numb their daily experience. 8. Drugs are relatively cheap and widely available. 9. The police do not enforce anti-drug laws strenuously – the Elite admit allowing organised crime to occur preferring it to disorganised crime. 10. A culture of immediate gratification. 11. The 'trauma of living' – see book 9 coming soon. 12. The former Soviets were heavily involved in international drug trades so as to permeate Western societies with drugs; with the intent to more easily take them down – that is a fact. Let's look at so-called 'Sensualism'.

The cult of Sensualism:

Casanova the famous occultist psychopath and 'womaniser' was not the only one but was amongst a small group, which included the infamous psychopath Count De Sade (interestingly both from 'upper' class backgrounds) who promoted the 'philosophical doctrine' that the senses are the sole source of knowledge. Although hedonistic cultures go way back into antiquity and always presage cultural collapse, we can see the modern roots of a climate favourable to addiction in Western human societies (Christian European model). They implicitly promote the unproven idea that addiction, per se, is not abnormal and unhealthy but is in fact the height of human experience. That this fantasy was promoted by psychopaths is no surprise. From 1813 onwards the cult of sensualism was known as being 'addiction to sensual indulgence'. ***NOTE: To a certain extent we have all been contaminated by these ideas.***

The ideas and changes, shamelessly promoted by all mass media that have altered and penetrated Western society have primed people to become addicts in times of stress. The social acceptance of drug use and of addiction as simply being part of 'growing up' is the biggest root cause of the addiction explosion. Now we know pretty much what caused it, the question is how do we get rid of it – on an individual basis? Curing society's ills is beyond the modest aims of this little book!

What follows are a number of key processes that will help you deprogramme addiction. This information will be mostly conveyed by a series of fictitious clients asking me for help. The cases presented will be based on composites of real people who wanted to be free of addiction. Over the course of your book we will cover the *addiction deprogramming process* from beginning to end – from interview stage to addiction busting interventions in hypnosis. They will be thorough, comprehensive and teach you the core principles which can be applied to anyone, with any addiction.

There is no point listing all the dangerous effects of tobacco, heroin, cocaine, marijuana etc. Not unless you need to know about possible withdrawals and how to handle them – the worst case of withdrawals I ever saw was with a smoker! Cocaine is easy to kick, marijuana is a bit of a bastard if someone is only 70% committed to quitting, nicotine cigarettes are the 'hardest' drug to come off of – why? Because the painful results can be delayed for years. Alcohol withdrawal only occurs in very severe drink dependency – the heavy drinker must cut down gradually; to do otherwise can kill them. Heavy drinking, not just drinking a glass or two of wine at night (a drink moderation session) is always caused by some kind of grief, loss or trauma. There is a lot of deep self-hate in severe alcoholism. In order to help addicts quit you often have to have several methods of boosting self-worth/esteem: in this book I'll show you how.

Although worry, anxiety and trauma often need to be addressed in ending addiction processes I cover these separately in my next and penultimate book 'Hypnotically annihilating anxiety'.

A note on the teen brain in relation to addiction propensities.

Most though not all of my addiction clients started their drug use in their teens. Why?

- The neocortex – the part of the brain responsible for executive functions like planning, attention, motivation, working memory, and impulse control is undergoing maturation.
- As a result of ongoing 'neuromaturation' teenage brains exhibit a set of consistently identifiable traits as they relate to the maturity of judgement. There are three in particular worth highlighting: 1. Increased novelty seeking. 2. Increased risk taking. 3. Increased desire to affiliate and interact with peers.
- A tendency toward high risk taking behaviour: Teens engage in all sorts of risk-taking behaviours because they have a heightened sensitivity to rewards — they've got a neuro-circuitry rich in dopamine and, in the case of males, testosterone. Dopamine is one of the key pleasure chemicals of the brain!
- Teens are more self-conscious than younger children or adults when they

think peers are watching — a consequence of their 'obsession' with social evaluation.

- Teens also make risky decisions in so-called 'hot' contexts — that is, where emotions are at stake or peers are present and social cognition is involved. In part this has to do with their hyper-responsive dopaminergic reward system and the prefrontal systems related to impulse control. Relatively speaking their impulse control is weaker – especially in 'the heat of the moment'.

- Teens have a weak sense of self in Western society – this predisposes them to media stereotypes of approved identity and behaviour.

To a certain extent an adult addict acts like a teenager. Do you think the people who make and sell drugs don't know this?

A reality check for those who think drugs are no big deal.

Russian news agency Tass 2nd December 2014: Drug addicts cost the Russian economy a whopping $82 billion a year! According to the Russian drugs control agency 65% of all crimes in the country are related to drugs. Russia is annually loosing up to 1.5 trillion rubles ($30.5 billion) of its GDP, as addicts spend an average of 4.5 billion Rubles ($91 million) a day on drugs. This is 1.5 times greater than Russia's defence spending, 3.5 higher than its health budget. Drugs have been declared a direct threat to the Russian economy. That's right, drugs are no big deal.

A brief note on using the scripts IF you haven't read my others books.

My first book, 'How to hypnotise anyone', (which has been US and UK number one bestseller for pretty much over a year at time of publishing) tells you how to speak like a hypnotist. For complete newcomers I will quickly tell you how to do so here...

- Slow your voice down.
- Speak in a relaxed tone when hypnotising someone.
- You can add more speed and energy but not too much when delivering the scripted 'interventions'.
- Squeeze the meaning of words out using voice tone: if you want someone to 'feel powerful' put a powerful tone behind those words etc. Say 'relax' in a soothing way. Emotions are hypnotic – read my other books and find out.
- Emphasise highlighted text (embedded commands) with a downward command tonality, as you would if telling someone kindly but firmly to close a door. Embedded commands are *incredibly* powerful.

You can also turn your head slightly – the subconscious/unconscious notices the difference and this marks out the message as important. These are subliminal communications that bypass resistance. *They even work when people are aware of them.*

Warning – if you are not a trained hypnotherapist you use these scripts at your own risk. I have tried to make them idiot proof but these days you never know!!! If in doubt play it safe, don't do it and seek professional help. No stupid risks please folks.

Quick tip section!

Tip 1: Drugs are parasites.

Think of a dirty little parasite of some kind. That's it. Some wretched creature: a tape worm, a lice, tick, mosquito etc. Maybe even a banker! Knock yourself out! That is what any real 'drug' is. The drug is not that addictive, usually. It is just a stimulus, the catalyst of an addiction process. Drugs need not be present in O.C.D (Obsessive Compulsive Disorder) but that has addictive elements. In hypnosis you need to persuade and re-associate the 'drug' with the idea of parasitism, not pleasure, kicks or 'friendship'. Once you do that, you leverage the person away from an abusive relationship toward a healthy one: with reality!

Tip 2: Simple dissociation of self and behaviour trick.

I covered this in book 3, 'Powerful hypnosis', I bring it up again now so that this book is comprehensive.

- Smoker etc. says, 'I am a smoker'. They identify self and behaviour as one.
- Take cushion.

- Throw cushion.
- Say, 'I just chucked that.' Am I a chucker?
- Client usually laughs – behaviour proven as dissociated. Simple.

Tip 3: How to check if an addict really wants to change unconsciously.

I have developed a system whereby I can pretty much help any addicted person who wants my assistance even if their conscious motivation is seemingly low. If you suspect you have a time waster however and don't need the money etc. (kidding! I think!) try this: it will make you seem highly ethical, which you are really. You place all the pressure on their unconscious in this manoeuvre. If they 'fail' the test, promise you'll help when they pass it because that will mean *they're* ready to change.

Pendulum test for junkies.

- You require 1 paper clip and 1 piece of thread.
- Tie clip to thread: voilà you have 'a pendulum'. This we use to talk to the subconscious.
- Tell the client to extend their arm,

take the pendulum between the forefinger and thumb in either hand, it don't matter which!

- *By now they'll be worried and wondering what you're doing. This is a pattern interrupt!*

- Say, *'I don't want to waste your time or money, nor mine for that matter if you are not motivated to change unconsciously. To find out if you are I need to ask your subconscious a simple question. I will say it first – I want you to say it to your own subconscious in your own mind next, don't say it out loud: 'Using a forward and back movement for yes and a side to side for no, can you tell me subconscious if you really want and are willing to change today? Do not try to move the string, let it move itself. Go!'*

Now you may save a whole lot of needless effort: I would use it with the real asshole clients.

NOTE: ideomotor signalling is actually problematic – the unconscious doesn't know everything! It is not omnipotent; sometimes it plays games, rebels, changes its mind all in one session.

Sometimes it doesn't know what it wants and YOU the hypnotist must tell it straight! Use ideomotor signalling rarely, with precision and caution. If a client comes to me to stop using drugs I BLAST the addiction away, no ifs of buts!

Tip 4: Don't expect clients to live like monks!

People like to be naughty and indulgent from time to time – we can't live like cloistered monks in the real world! If a client will only let go of one addiction – settle for that. They'll come back when they're ready to let go of others too. Tell your clients we all need a few vices just to keep life fun! Tell them you do not want them to live like a monk and behave 'perfectly' because that's not possible in this world! This will help you come across as someone who can demonstrate common-sense. It will make you 'approachable' rather than the all-knowing therapist myth. Yeah – like you never tried anything naughty in your lifetime. What's that I can smell? Oh it's bullsh*t!

Tip 5: Never play high status with addicts.

People prone to addictions are natural rebels – if you get on a social superior, superior morality trip with them YOU WILL FAIL! Treat them as equals. Normalise what they do. Tell them most people do it. Act as though you have an 'each to their own' mentality even if you don't. Who cares what you think anyway? You are a f***ing health professional not a professional, condescending, self-righteous moralist. They are paying you to help them not judge them. Who made you perfect anyway!

Treat ALL clients as you would ideally like to be treated in similar circumstances: make light of it, offer optimism of 'cure' and most importantly - deliver results.

Addiction case 1: My first dramatic breakthrough session - authoritarian-esque style.

Good hypnotic interventions negotiate with the subconscious. In the following script which 'cured' (total permanent removal of all unwanted behaviour – 'symptoms' don't interest me) a professional single parent woman in her 30's of both a regular nicotine cigarette and an after work, evening marijuana habit. Left alone by her parents in the evening as a child she had always been rewarded with a treat, such as a piece of chocolate or a biscuit. By going along with such neglect she was a 'good girl' according to her totally irresponsible middle class parents. This early operant conditioning unwittingly set up a pattern that said in effect – if you are unhappy have a treat. This lady was lonely, divorced – she needed a new husband or a boyfriend – her needs for companionship, esteem, positive regard, intimacy, her desire to be thought attractive, sex etc. were not being met. Drugs tried to fill the gap – but pseudo-satisfactions never last. She was in just the right 'place' to change. The timing was right and so the tricks I used below worked – in many cases they won't.

Due to my original training I started off using more aversive anti-drug techniques which I don't use at all now. My 2nd and more successful strategy was quite authoritarian. The 'telling off' of the subconscious intervention below directly says to the subconscious – *'Don't do that anymore it's really stupid and dangerous: it won't work. Do healthier alternatives x, y and z instead.'* In addition I threw in an NLP swish pattern just before waking the lady up from hypnotic trance – see 'Powerful hypnosis' for details of this. I started off with an NLPesque pattern before the direct hypnosis (see below); however I do not use it anymore. I am not a big fan of NLP but sometimes the patterns do work with oodles of other stuff ladled on top – they can be good nudges. This pattern, which I have altered, I include below for you...

The direct stop smoking script.

(Deep hypnosis assumed)

'In a moment I will say the word 'relax' and you can go 10 times deeper into hypnotic trance feeling wonderful...'Rel-ax!' That's it. That's a great place to start the process of ***CHANGE!***

Step 1: NLPesque 'non-junkie' belief pattern for all drug addiction/unwanted habits etc.

- Think of a very strong belief you have. See an image that represents that belief... *(Allow about 5-6 seconds processing time.)* Notice its qualities – what are they? Is it bright, bold and colourful? Is it big and close? Is it small or far away? Are there any sounds or smells? Notice all of its unique qualities fully...*(Allow about 7-10 seconds processing.)*

- Think of something you desire but DON'T act on. See an image that fully represents that. We all have areas in life where we ***control certain desires.*** What are this belief's qualities? Again: is it bright and colourful? Is it small or big? far away or close? Any sounds, smells? Is it located in a different place in your mind? If so note where. Notice all the unique qualities of this belief and how you represent it to yourself.

- Think of a situation where you have the option to smoke *(x, y, z – drug of no choice – nicotine cigarettes, joints etc.)* Move that image away and change all the qualities of that image automatically into the exact same ones as the thing you desire but don't act on. Lock it in! Great! *(Allow 1-2 seconds only – move on quick!)*

- See yourself not acting upon it: ***a happy, free, healthy non-smoker*** *(etc.)* ***now.*** *(Again max 3-5 secs or so.)*

- Take that image of you not acting upon

the craving – ***being a happy, healthy non-smoker from now on – forever!*** Now, very quickly at the speed of thought, move it off into the distance and snap it back into the qualities and position of that strong belief automatically! *(1 second pause!)* Great! It's locked in place permanently! You can take this act as a sign and a signal that ***you believe in that place and with those qualities of thought that are appropriate that <u>you are a non-smoker now</u> and for the rest of your life!*** The changes have been made, lock them in unconsciously and keep them permanently! Fan-tastic!

<u>Step 2: Direct negotiation with the subconscious to stop smoking anything.</u>

(Embedded commands that follow aren't needed – I put them in to drive certain points home! Experiment!)

'Now once again I am speaking to the part that is in control of this process...the subconscious mind...I'd first of all like to take this opportunity to thank you on this person's behalf for protecting them, looking after them and any and all positive changes you've ever made in their life. Thank you so much for that.

Up until this moment you had been creating the

old, 'perceived' essential pattern of smoking. You had created cravings, desires for cigarettes, for marijuana joints etc. – that former wish to smoke. I know that consciously and unconsciously, now...that you had a series of very good reasons for doing so; otherwise you wouldn't have done what you once did. That was the past pattern and you couldn't have maintained that any better if you tried.

The time has come where you have consciously and unconsciously reached the 'enough is enough moment' – ***you've had enough*** of the old ways of being, have you not? The time is now perfectly right for you to ***stop smoking completely, once and for all, now...***You realise at all levels of mentation, of information processing that the old habit of smoking that used to occur automatically in response to certain cues, certain experiences is not what is optimally healthy for this unique individual – it doesn't make life genuinely easier in any area of their life anymore, if it really ever did.

There are better ways to get your genuine needs met, and at a very deep unconscious level you know this. Once a tool is worn out, past its prime, ***you get a new set of tools. Now,*** there are better, more functional, healthier ways to achieve those positive intentions without the negative side-effects of the past unwanted behaviour. Improvements can occur physically – you'll ***feel fitter and be able to breathe more naturally and easy.*** You will be able to ***relax more naturally,*** to ***put things in their proper perspective,*** you'll ***feel happier and more in control in general.*** Certain changes will occur mentally, emotionally - and that just feels great to know doesn't it?

Your finances will improve as you'll have more money to spend as you wish, or save for something special – you no longer give your hard earned money to that thief who stole it. A friend doesn't, would never steal from you. And don't be surprised if your relationships don't improve too, in ways perhaps that you cannot readily foresee that will surprise and delight you, now.

It is time now, better now to ***be a non-smoker from this moment on, now...***
It is no good being an ex-smoker - that's for others if they want. You the subconscious can powerfully ensure that ***this person is a non-smoker*** because they experience ***absolutely no cravings, obsessing or withdrawals at all, no desire for that which is in the past, now.***

As this person finds it ***easy to think for yourself and make your own decisions*** no matter what others do...being with friends or anyone else for that matter who still chose to smoke is fine, easy, no bother at all; others are entitled to do as they wish and ***YOU DO LIKEWISE.*** That is not what you do any...more, now...past associations in any sensory modality have no power, no effect, there are no unpleasant feelings – ***no problem whatsoever!*** If someone offers you a cigarette you can ***politely yet confidently decline things you don't want.*** You'll find just the right ways and words without effort – and that's a nice thing to be sure of, is it not?

Picking up, accepting a cigarette is laughable, silly, absurd – it seems so alien that you know, really know that to do so would be ludicrous for you and it doesn't happen. It's not a part of your reality anymore. It's just not what you chose to do.

Every time you ***experience these new healthy patterns, these improved responses, now*** – your subconscious will give you a reward – a set of marvellous feelings that make you feel good as you confidently take this new path in life – you ***feel great being a non-smoker*** and you like it that way.

You know this is true because you deserve these changes – you are a person of tremendous worth and value, many people love and appreciate you, you are esteemed more than you know. Good people deserve to feel healthy and free. As a healthy person you find sensible ways to look after your health in improved ways. You know the importance of treating yourself too and having fun. You have all the poise and total self-belief you need – your subconscious always aids you powerfully in all your best efforts and that's that.

Adjustments are now occurring at a very deep level and being finalised. Attitudes can change. Thoughts can appropriately alter. Lifestyle choices can improve. Perceptions, patterns, persistence and willpower are enhanced. You can ***go beyond those old limiting habits, now!***

Natural changes occur in arousal and relaxation responses to certain triggers and cues. You have an inborn ability that you reconnect to now to – ***feel good natural feelings naturally, now!***

Book of beliefs sub-module.

(*If clients lack belief in the ability to change you can try the following. A more powerful NLPesque pattern for changing beliefs is included later.)*

Imagine there is a book in that place in your mind where you believe things to be true…it's called 'Your beliefs!' It's such a beautiful book. Open it; and as you do, you'll find as you flick through, a blank page: take a magic looking, old fashioned pen or quill nearby and dip it in the golden ink or some other colour you associate with positive certainty and write in this belief that you told me you wanted – 'I fully believe that I am and will be perfectly fine without tobacco and marijuana; I know how to ***feel fine*** without any artificial external aids *(etc.)' (5-7 sec pause)*...Great! Now close the book with a good feeling. A knowing feeling that ***important shifts have occurred, now.***

Finalisation process.

Communications are adapting...Powerful new associations being formed and strengthened... Re-associations occur...Re-organisations of already existing subconscious structures take place. Subtle, appropriate adjustments can happen...Anything and everything else that needs to change to help you get real satisfaction of your deepest needs occurs right now! ***You are a non-smoker from this day forth*** and it feels magic! You are free and know it, really know it! You feel happy, healthy – in mind, body, soul! You ***feel so confident in yourself,*** your life and in your capacity to ***achieve all your deeply desired goals!*** Past positive ways returned – yet enhanced – grown stronger, better than ever! A higher level of functioning, maturity with a clean bill of health! The subconscious finalises all these significant change now! As quickly as possible in the next few seconds! Only ever changing in life-enhancing, positive, healthy ways... NOOOOO-OOOW! You can access your own associative matrix to uncover improved responses that can be permanently structured into better ways of being and living that please you most, now.

(3-5 second pause...)

Brilliant! You are doing really well!

Step 3: Handling cravings with positive associations.

(I outlined one method of getting rid of cravings in book 6, 'Crafting hypnotic spells' – you can try the following if you think it will help. Give sufficient processing time after the questions and tasks etc.; anywhere from 5 to 20 seconds will be appropriate, use your judgement.)

- Become aware of your own process for handling cravings or desires, tough periods etc....What do you do?
- Can you recall a time you had a strong craving or strong desire and just be aware

step by step what you did to ensure you didn't smoke?

- How did being successful in handling that time, of managing those cravings, those desires make you feel?
- Did you feel pride? A good feeling? Powerful? Did you feel very successful?
- Have you ever felt that way about anything else in your life, even if for just a few brief moments?
- Just be in that experience as fully as possible, now. A time you felt that wonderful feeling, totally powerful, totally successful, totally proud. See it through your own eyes. Hear the sounds through your own ears, ***feel those wonderful sensations in your body.*** Intensify them now, let those feelings grow and build! That's it! Now say a word to yourself and/or press your finger and thumb together to bring back these feelings at will, whenever you need them. We'll call this your control trigger! *(Sometimes this phase requires 3 repetitions in total to link the new associations strongly.)*
- Now see yourself out in your wonderful free future for a couple of days, a couple of weeks, months, years as ***a powerful,***

successful, proud non-smoker, now... taking these wonderful feelings with you! Use your trigger to boost the feelings even more if it helps.

- Go through some times, some situations where in the past you might have smoked, but do those things now as a non-smoker keeping, intensifying each time the proud, powerful, successful, positive emotional state. As you ***feel those feelings during that experience*** use your trigger as they reach a peak. I'll be quiet while you practise that. *(Hypnotist's note: you can be silent for a whole minute.)* Perfect.

- Now whenever you want those feelings use your trigger and fire them off smothering any old desires completely, now. And this is so.'

(With all addiction sessions with clients I include the physiological withdrawal pattern which I invented from book 3, 'Powerful hypnosis'. With this client I didn't do it – I was lucky she had no bad withdrawal response; from bitter experience I learnt this was not always the case. After care with clients is a must. Begin wake up procedure of choice etc. Note: I bash the subconscious from so many angles its defences cannot resist – as I have said in at least one other book, therapy is war!)

If you chose the right interventions I promise you – addiction deprogramming is alarmingly easy. When confronted by real world people with addictions (don't use the word 'addict' with a client – do not hypnotically label them with a static noun!) I suggest you use the interventions in this book and others I've written as you see fit. Just because I have used them one way doesn't mean they'll work for the unique person before you. You must use your 'clinical' judgement. This takes a bit of practise before becoming streamlined.

Addiction case 2: Stop smoking for good – re-associations, negotiations, suggestion!

Another lady, several years after the case above. She had been to see me before and we'd made progress. She had quit cigarettes for about 6 months. But a series of life stressors had popped out of nowhere. She had grown up in a school where you where bullied if you did not fit in and go along with the crowd!!! In other words, for her subconscious – conformity of any kind had generalised into having survival value. She knew she could quit – her problem now was, she had to stay quit for good! The object of the session was *permanency.* I needed to do several things to knock this problem on the head. I call the process...

The deprogramming smoking addiction permanently script.

(Deep hypnosis assumed)

Step 1: Reinforcing the desire to stop smoking forever!

(It all seems so conversational – your embeds are doing the work!)

'I know that you want to ***remain nicotine free permanently...***In order to do so... you need to ***have unconscious motivation***

to stop, now...We know that you can ***quit*** because you have stopped smoking before... I know that you have found the motivation to ***stop doing certain things*** in the past... In order to ***stop for good*** you need to... fully ***become a genuine non-smoker, now...***When you follow that path toward health so many improvements are possible...We do things for a while and then we realise ***that habit is not a part of you...***It is something you did formerly and then ***you just outgrow stuff...***It's really time to ***just stop*** doing what you no longer really wish to do...

I could talk to you about the damage that smoking does but that won't really help...I'm sure you know more about that than me...You can know however that it only takes just 2 days for ***that drug to be out of your system*** physically...So you can know that the assumed power of ***that habit is much weaker*** than you knew...In fact it ***grows less and less potent by the second until - <u>it's gone completely...</u>***Have you heard that saying '**Give up** the ghost?' Well that's what that unwanted habit is doing, ***now...*** *(Hypnotic coding: see book 2.)*

<u>*Step 2: Mentally rehearse new patterns.*</u>

Take a moment to imagine times, places, people you might be with when you might have

smoked in the past...but see yourself as a non-smoker, not an ex-smoker – ***you really are a non-smoker and that is your new reality...***Just mentally rehearse, at a very deep level, going through a few times, say 3 or 4 in which you can see yourself confidently acting as a non-smoker in all ways...I'll be quiet for a full minute while you ***practise this reality.***

(Do so...)

Step 3: Evoking re-associations and facing reality.

Excellent! Aren't you sick of being robbed? Aren't you sick of being poisoned? Aren't you sick of being bullied? Aren't you sick of that damage that that drug and those drug dealers have caused? Actually consider these realities for a moment – imagine them fully if you wish, if that helps you ***alter your perceptions and old associations, unconsciously*** on certain matters.

(Considering things in hypnosis is a highly focused process – hint! Pause for between 20 -30 seconds to allow processing.)

Step 4: Parasitic poison reframing.

Smoking is not your friend – it never was: do you know, really know what a genuine parasite is? It is something that lives off of you. It uses you to suit its own ends. Sometimes it acts as if it's helping you. It cons you that you need it. And that means it lies to you – deception is not a good basis for any relationships, wouldn't ***you agree...*** (?)

When the reality is you need to ***get your genuine needs met naturally in reality...*** It's time to ***stop believing in the fantasy*** that smoking is anything other than what it is, and you know deep down, really know just what that is, do you not?

That habit had been oppressing you systematically. Robbing you of your health. Robbing you of your freedom. Robbing you of opportunity and longevity. Perhaps you can ***start to feel very, very differently*** in the light of these new, more realistic appraisals and perspectives that help...

Imagine how much better that mind and body will function...You'll ***breathe more easily and feel clean and purified...That parasitic pollution is gone, now.*** At a profoundly deep level of information processing...in a place of wisdom beyond past programmed-in illusions is the knowledge of exactly how and why you should and do ***feel very differently about nicotine cigarettes***....Your deepest unconscious feelings and associations to that past stimulus and the expectations of that poisonous stimulus can ***radically alter, now.*** And this change can and will occur outside of your curious awareness...And that kind of trust can be so comforting...The comfort of ***your positive – change!***

Step 5: Changing identities, time and messages.

Have you ever done something and you seemed so wrapped up in the moment of it? And then days, weeks, months and eventually a whole load of years passed and you came to realise that what once *seemed* so important had diminished in significance significantly...So much so that ***that habit seemed something of so long, long ago...like memories of times past.***

And thankfully that is the reality of ***your being a non-smoker*** and taking ***that profound identity change, now*** and ***total belief in that change*** into the deepest part of your true identity, yes, even to that place beyond your name...that's it!

You no longer listen to the old messages; it's as if they fade, fade, fade to silence... You have outgrown certain places, people, things throughout your life...That's the process of ***maturing...***Of discovering your true identity beyond passing habits. Sometimes we try stuff on and some of it doesn't fit and we ***stop it.*** And in doing so we are free to ***make new choices, find new solutions.***

The human body has an amazing and simply not understood capacity to ***self-heal...Now,*** the exact mechanisms are unknown consciously...Won't it be amazing to notice the positive changes... (?) To know, really know that ***you have stopped for good.*** That all areas of your life have benefited. You ***feel different mentally.*** You ***believe new things*** about yourself. You ***feel differently emotionally*** about what was. You feel emotionally stronger, more motivated, your total commitment to ***maintain these gains permanently as part of your deepest identity*** is rooted in the wellspring of who you are. You make better decisions daily...Your finances and relationships improve...And more and more and more...

Step 6: Ending a real-hate-shun-ship.

Have you ever had a friend that you grew apart from...? Just somehow and in some way...you grew cold on that person and ***you ended that relationship...***And what seemed sad turned out to be one of the best things that happened to you, did it not? Did...it...not? ***Quit*** feeling sorry for what doesn't deserve your sympathy... I know you can do it, each and both of you know you can and did and have...And that's that.

Step 7: Advanced level parts negotiation.

(Although we are dealing with smoking; you can use this with many drugs/addictions etc. ***There is no doubt about it – the secret to really effective addiction busting is to carry out parts negotiation work.*** *Addictions are maintained by a 'gang' of unconscious functions all pulling in the wrong direction. They have been conned by the fantasy that the drug of no choice can fulfil certain needs BUT they also know that these needs were NEVER fulfilled; this is your point of leverage as a therapist. This leaves the parts open to negotiation. You are not taking the addiction away and leaving nothing. A void won't do. The parts must be convinced that the new way is better, will really create genuine satisfaction of needs and therefore work long-term. What follows is but one way to negotiate, another follows in the section on cocaine addiction – both processes being my modified forms of so-called 'Ego state therapy'; the difference is that my versions will succeed! You can create a 'place of real agreement' etc. in the mind and have the negotiations take place there. You don't have to but let's do it...)*

In the following we talk to these 'parts':

- **Younger experimenting self (teen fool with no developed neocortex!)**
- **'The Maintainer': self that maintains habit.**
- **Wiser adult self. (This is the 'objective self'. It alone has a rounded perspective on all the issues.)**
- **'The Innovator' or Creative self.**

Note: I do not set up ideomotor signals (finger wiggles) etc. I find it is better to assume success; if you ask for unconscious feedback the unconscious can muck around and play silly buggers. Just take them through the process and assume it's all going A-okay: in my experience introducing any doubt of success can stop it happening. When you see 'NFH' in the text it means 'Note for hypnotist' not 'No f*ing hope!'**

(NFH: when you give a client a task, allow sufficient processing time.)

1. I'd like you to imagine a place in your mind where only agreement is possible – a place we'll call 'The place of real agreement'. Whenever all the parts of ourselves are in full alignment and pulling in the same

direction we must ***be congruent at a deep level.*** I have no idea what that place is like; it's yours, so you do! Whatever comes to mind spontaneously is correct.

2. Make sure that the parts that we invite to help you ***stop smoking permanently*** have somewhere to sit.

3. Now anyone's unconscious mind is made of differing parts and functions that have different tasks and roles if you like. These parts that you invite simply symbolise these things. With that in mind, I would like to talk to your deepest parts.

4. Can you invite the part that once made you smoke – that first tried that out, to this place of healing, change and agreement? Just imagine them taking a seat somewhere. Always remembering ***you are in charge of this changing process*** – I am just a guide. *(3 – 5 sec pause.)*

5. Good. The first thing I'd like you to do *so and so (client's name)* is to simply inform this part in no uncertain terms what you know about all the dangers, the risks, the very real costs of that old habit ***you'd like to change.*** You now know more than they did. We always make decisions on the best

information we have available. Inform them of what you now know from your mature, more adult perspective. This will help them ***operate from an updated level of more realistic information*** than they had in the past. New information can help you change. Facts alter things. I'll be quiet for 20 seconds or so while you do that. You have all the time you need in trance. *(Do so...)*

6. Great! Now, it is important that you really let them know that you understand fully that you know they had a positive reason back in that time and place for engaging in that old behaviour. I'll be quiet for a bit while you do so. *(Pause 10 secs or so.)*

7. Good! Let them know that those former reasons are out of date - they are in-valid now. I'll be quiet again while you do so. *(Pause 10 secs or so.)*

8. Okay! Can you also let them know that because it's time to ***change now*** all the parts of you will help and support them in this change? With support all ***healthy change is easy!*** *(Pause for 10 secs or so.)*

9. Good! Can you assure them that during this process we will help them find other, perhaps one in particular, perhaps several

better ways to actually satisfy those valid and real reasons for first engaging in that former behaviour pattern that are healthy, positive and beneficial by asking the creative part to lend a hand? *(5-7 seconds should do it.)*

10. Excellent! Can you now ask that younger self if it is willing to help you in changing? ***Stopping that old unhealthy behaviour, now.*** *(Wait for up to 10 secs – you may get a nod or smile. Assume it has worked – I have never had an instance where it didn't. If you get some signal that there is a problem, it may be that the part wants the new choices now. Assure it that soon you'll ask the creative part to generate new ways etc.)*

11. With all this in mind and knowing that your adult self will always aid you – that in fact all the parts of who you truly are will assist, help and support you – please ask that younger you if they would be willing to ***unconsciously disconnect from that old set of reasons now.*** *(Wait for 7-10 secs etc.)*

12. *(Symbolic act of dissociation from habit)* As soon as you have a yes response I want you to imagine something that uniquely symbolises ***this disconnection taking place*.*** It might involve pushing

something away, removing something from something else, throwing away your last pack of cigarettes/empty bottles, removing a plug from a socket, putting something in the wastebasket etc. *(Suggest the symbology of the disconnect come from the client – if you provide it, and you can, it will still probably work most of the time. However it might not tap into their unique way of representing this process: and that's the key to success in hypnosis! Allow 10 secs or so – you'll just get a sense when it's done.)* **NFH: Later in this book I will show you a separate pattern to do this – you can add it here if you wish.*

13. *(Scrooge pattern variant – in the next part of this process you show the person what could happen if they don't change. I offered a way to do this is in one of my other books. Here is a slightly different approach. It offers a warning which will be vividly experienced in trance of taking the wrong path!)* Great – you are doing brilliantly. But before we carry on, I want you to seriously consider something first. I would like for you to imagine a possible future. It hasn't happened. But it might if you don't ***change habits and direction, now.*** Visualise a time in the future – with you looking at an older you, dissociated from that image, say 15-20 years ahead in

which you have continued to smoke cigarettes/drink heavily etc. Look at that you and how their health is suffering IF you fail to ***take this opportunity.*** *(Give them some processing time.)*

14. See and notice how that you *is* suffering. Do they have problems breathing? Are they tired and unfit? How badly have they aged? How rough does the skin look? Are they undergoing any kind of medical procedures? Notice all the possible effects of not ***changing now.*** *(Let them view it etc. I dissociate people, some therapists don't – 1. I don't want someone experiencing a lung disorder in trance thanks!!! 2. When you dissociate a client, they can view things objectively AND it sends a signal to the unconscious that this possibility is being disconnected/dissociated from – that is, it won't happen! I am only doing this because it is a follow up session – the person must realise the danger of addiction!)*

15. Your wiser you has some helpful advice – ***listen intently*** to what your wiser you has to say, it is very important and will help you at this stage in the process. *(Be quiet for about 10 secs etc. and pray their 'wiser you', whoever he/she/it is, knows*

his/her stuff!!!)

16. Okay that's great! *So and so* (client's name): now is the time to make a promise to yourself, a vow, an oath if you like, that ***that possible future never happens to you, now.*** *(Throw an embed in to help! Also 'that' = dissociated, see book 2, 'Mastering hypnotic language'.)*

17. Can you invite that part of you that maintains that habit you want to change? This part is the part that does everything you needed to keep that going back then. It motivated you to buy cigarettes come what may. It rationalised that old behaviour pattern. Just let it take a seat somewhere *(a beat or so)*. Good. I'd like to thank that part for you, for all it did on your behalf. It did that job very well. Now I would like to assure that part that we are going to take care of those very good reasons for which you once did those things. But can you ***change sides, now*** and very powerfully and strongly ***help this person*** in their fantastic goal of ***being a non-smoker*** etc. for the rest of their life? I'd like *you* to thank this part and ask for its help too. *(Pause for 10 seconds or so etc. for it to agree – it always does.)*

18. Great! Now I would like you to invite the powerful creative part of you that comes up with all those solutions for you to take a seat. *(A beat...)* Good. This part is so good at generating new ideas, things, thoughts, plans, insights, intuitions, feelings even, and envisages things in order to help you – that's its role! It does it very well. Some people call it the gifted part, the innovator *(NFH: flatter it!)*. I would like to thank it for all it's done for you and you can take the time to offer your appreciation to it too. *(A beat etc.)* Good. I would like to ask that part to ***generate some new, better, healthier alternatives*** to smoking/eating too much etc. that genuinely satisfies those essential needs that the old ways *tried* to fulfil *(implied – they failed!)*. There are so many behaviours to choose from. You can ask that part to help too. And once you've done that – I'll be quiet while it can ***create new choices...***It might select one or several; it's entirely up to that part of you. *(Pause for 30 seconds or so.)*

19. Next, can you ask the wonderful creative part of you if it would now be willing to try out one new behaviour; to ***experiment*** - a new alternative, one after another or several if it prefers until the best one or ones are found? And once it has done that

for you, thank it for its help. *(Quiet for 30 secs or so again to allow processing, which usually in my experience happens quite quickly.)*

20. Thank you – you are doing really well! Okay it's now time for all of these ***parts*** to ***integrate*** into a fully congruent, motivated, unified non-smoking/drinking/drug using etc. whole, ***now.*** *(Pause a beat)* Perfect!!!

21. Now you can ***feel this unified power*** as you know deep down that ***you have changed.*** You have that knowing feeling that this is so. Turn that powerful non-smoking feeling into a colour! That's it! Let it spread from where it starts all through your body! Let it get brighter and brighter and as it does ***this feeling grows*** more and more powerful! Great! You can take this act as a sign and a signal that ***significant changes were made,*** haven't we?

22. You can ***relax and feel strengthened*** with the very certain knowledge that ***all the parts of you are pulling in the same direction determined to succeed!*** All the parts of you offer support and encouragement consciously if appropriate and unconsciously too, from now on. You can hear them offering

encouragement! ***Feel that support, strength and power!*** With all parts of you working together like a purposeful team - you *are* powerful! You'll find that in such a frame of mind you can do anything healthy, positive and realistic that you truly desire to do! That's a nice thing to know isn't it?

23. And this time ***ALL THE PARTS OF YOU CAN INTERGRATE INTO TOTAL ALIGNMENT!*** Per-fect! You are a non-smoker, you know this, you desire this, you believe this and it feels amazing doesn't it!? United this way you ***feel strong, determined and resolute*** that ***you achieve this worthwhile goal.*** Remembering that all parts are unconditionally giving you the total support and security you need, they can get back to doing what they do on your behalf, unconsciously. Great! We've almost finished this stage in the process and you are doing so well!

24. Now we talked about this earlier – there was a need that the old behaviour served in its way. Can you let that need come to your awareness now somehow? *(Pause for 10-15 seconds as your client receives some internal message...)* Good. You now know that ***you have better ways to***

satisfy that genuine need. You now know that your creative part has already found and is finding improved and healthy alternatives to ***get that need met positively, now.*** All parts of you are integrated unconsciously now. All parts can find positive, healthy and better ways to ***satisfy that need responsibly.*** You have precisely the right mind-set to succeed and it feels good knowing that, does it not? As a consequence ***you feel unstoppable, unbeatable*** – a powerful alliance has been made that changes your life in ways that can surprise and delight you, now!!! Imagine that new, non-smoker you! In the achievement of this goal you are invincible!

25. ***Dissociated rehearsal:*** Now, it's time to practise your success. I want you to imagine 3 times – one after the other, in which in former times you may have smoked/used drug 'X'/drank too much etc. But on these occasions now, you find yourself ***using a new alternative*** choice that your creative self-developed/found. As though watching a movie...see yourself going through each time as a totally confident non-smoker/moderate drinker etc. See yourself calm and happy. Everything is how it should be. Look at the power in that you over there – see them

dealing with anything that arises successfully! Just as you wish. I'll be quiet for a full minute while you rehearse that success! In trance you have all the time you need. *(Do so...)*

26. ***Associated rehearsal:*** Great! Now going through those times again, I want you to step into the memories and ***experience this new non-smoking reality*** from the inside...That's it! Feel your power! Feel the ease of new choices! Feel how much better it feels to ***live your life this new way.*** You have reconnected to who you really are! You have taken back control! You have the power to succeed. And that that's a nice thing to be and feel 100% certain of isn't it? It feels wonderful doesn't it? I'll be quiet while you do that. *(Again give them a minute!)*

27. Brilliant! You can take this act as a sign and a signal that ***in the core of who you are you are a non-smoker/free of drug x etc. forever!*** And it feels brilliant!

You could leave the session there but I use my 'overwhelming firepower principle' and bash the subconscious into submission; in the nicest way possible! I firmly directionalise the person's brain on the right path using repetition of themes etc. and emphasis. If you prefer you do not have to summon parts etc.: you can simply have a client 'get the sense' of them.

Stage 8. Stopping smoking permanently summation suggestions.

Okay you are doing so well. I just have a few more things to say to sum up and then we're done.

It was a great decision to ***get rid of that old habit once and for all.*** You can be justly proud about all the amazing changes you have made. ***Removing that from your life*** boosts your health, longevity and so much more. The day has come so that from now on ***you are a non-smoker...***We all reach a point when we know ***this is the time to change...***When you placed the appointment you knew ***this is the time...***Consciously and unconsciously ***you've made up your mind to be free*** from now on permanently and for the rest of your long and much happier life...You feel calmer, more relaxed and confident than you have in some time...That's the result when you ***stop smoking forever, now...***At some point I know, and each and both of you know, that ***you are not smoking anymore...***Your body and mind feel healthier, your lungs work better, sooner than you expect...The mind can generalise from this success...What else can you do? What do you really want to do? What better more rewarding and fulfilling ways will you fill your time with? The deepest levels of your mind find ways to ***boost your 100% resolve, willpower and determination to succeed lifelong.*** Your creative part is generating solutions to problems...It is helping you ***find much better ways to get your genuine needs satisfied*** than ever before...as a consequence your whole life improves for the better...

Take this opportunity to realise how great this feels...***you are completely free of that habit, you are now a non-smoker...***As you take an in breath these words become a tangible reality in your experience ***in control now...***Emotions better...mind better...smelling better...parts working together...body better... the ***old connections and associations are gone...***The process of fully returning health has begun...you experience a knowing feeling* of success...Enjoy the new ***fitness, vitality and energy you experience...sticking firmly with this great decision, noooo-oooooow!'***

*(*You may have noticed me using a term above now and again – 'knowing feelings'; these are feelings we all have that so and so is true/false etc. In hypnosis we can deliberately elicit this state to lock in changes: after all if you feel something is so, then it is! I developed this after studying the neuroscience of hypnosis and writing my last book, 'Escaping cultural*

hypnosis'.)

<u>*Analysis.*</u>

1. <u>*Changing associations step – 1-6.*</u>

The first 6 steps are really just 1 big step. That script starts to alter the client's perceptions of smoking/addiction etc. In order to get change we basically reframe what smoking 'means' to the client.

2. <u>*Parts negotiation step - 7.*</u>

Broadly speaking the above process can be broken into the following formula. Again: **Parts negotiations are the most important intervention in addiction therapy** – in my experience they make or break success AND alone will often do the work.

Phase 1: Set up a 'place of agreement' and contact the original drug experimenting part. *(A part rooted in the past.)*

Phase 2: Symbolically dissociate from old behaviour.

Phase 3: Dissociated <u>*possible*</u> negative future review.

Phase 4: Contact the part that maintains the habit. *(A part rooted in present concerns.)*

Phase 5: Engage the creative part to generate solutions – it is vital that the client take responsibility for problem solving. You are teaching them essential life skills that generate more than creativity; they create independence. *Getting the power of the creative part on board is vital to any hypnotic intervention.*

Phase 6: Integrate parts and offer support etc.

Phase 7: 'Future pace'/rehearse success and the FEELINGS associated with it. ***To successfully persuade you need to change associations and feelings.***

3. *Reinforcing change step - 8.*

A series of pretty basic suggestions to consolidate changes. We're done! Give post hypnotic command for future trance etc. and start wake up procedure. This is explained in other books and detailed in your appendix.

Reality check post script: a word on 'E-cigarettes'.

So-called E-cigarettes are being touted as the greatest thing since sliced bread as I write: an addiction without consequences! Don't you believe it! Prediction: E-cigarettes WILL lead to health problems. Already one source is claiming that they allow MORE carcinogens *(cancer causing chemicals)* into the body. Don't say you weren't warned...If it looks too good to be true...

2 Bonus modules.

I have also used the two following, small modules to help addiction clients in the past. They are mini scripts – I usually throw them in near the end but you must use your best judgement. They may be used with clients in a first session; however I tend to use them for 2nd or what I call 'top up' sessions after a period of success and 'relapse'.

Reconnecting to old positive associations script.

'Remember a really good time when you were feeling good etc. without X *(drug of no choice)*. Look at that you who looked healthy; notice how good you looked, your skin tone improved, health and energy boosted, ***feeling truly optimistic and in control,*** a time you felt genuinely good about yourself.

Step into that healthy you who already did it! Learn from yourself intuitively what you did but ***do it better.*** You know what to do! How good do you feel from this perspective? How good was it to ***re-experience that, now*** ? Take the learnings from that past time and renew them, re-access them, re-associate to them, unconsciously, now!'

Before you had problem X.

'For so many years you lived without X *(drugs, drink, porn etc.)*. You weren't born that way. It was something you learnt and unlearnt, haven't you? All those long years of living healthily, doing all those things that children, maybe teenagers or as an adult from time to time do enjoyably without X. You knew how to ***feel good naturally*** – you just did it, without artificial help. Like joyful children who ***feel the joy of living from the simple things,*** the pleasure of this world, of tangible reality; these learnings are there within you – ***re-access them, unconsciously, now...***do it better than before, haven't you?'

(People have all the natural uppers and downers they need to feel good without drugs. They live in such artificial societies that synthetic pleasure appears natural. People who claim that 'primitive' people did drugs and so it is natural are idiots – those tribes started drug taking once their societies were adversely impacted upon by Westernisation and its standardisation processes; that is, as their cultures were being destroyed! For more powerful pleasure elicitation scripts which can be VERY helpful with addictions, see book 6 in my series, 'Crafting hypnotic spells' which covers pleasure and hypnosis extensively.

Additional note: perfect grammar etc. is not required nor wholly desirable in hypnotic work...)

Addiction case 3: The case of the Cocaine Kid!

This section covers a 1st and 2nd session intervention with a young man in his mid-twenties who was abusing cocaine, or should that be being abused by it? He also had a gambling addiction. I will cover these two sessions from interview stage onward to describe the whole 'curative' process I took him through. He remains drug free and happy to this day. But first let's meet the fellow I jokingly call, 'The Cocaine Kid!' He is an individual who sums up the whole f**ked post-millennial generation. You've heard of 'Generation X'; we'll the young people who come to see me I call 'Generation F'd' – take a wild guess why.

The interview.

A typical young working class man turns up at my house. He is basically a nice sort. Not very bright but good-hearted. His life is a mess. He likes football (soccer), the religion of the modern Englishman. He started using coke when going 'clubbing' (night clubs) as a teenager with his equally dopey friends. What follows is my usual 'hypno-quiz for addictions questionnaire'.

1. *Q: How are things at the moment?* A: 'Life is fantastic!' (He's lying; he is doing

'robo-speech': not thinking, just word emission in a social context...)

2. *Q: Okay. What do you do for a living and do you enjoy it?* A: He works in a 'maintenance role' for a transport service provider in the UK. He says he has no stressors at work. I believe him. In this area of life he is quite happy and settled. It's a good working class job with some security etc.

3. *Q: What's your living situation? You married, single, any kids?* A: Living with parents. Cocaine is preventing him from moving on in life, getting a girlfriend and having children which he really wants. **Missing needs identified – need for a close and intimate relationship. Sexual frustration. Feels trapped.** The key need that I find is being missed out on with about 90-95% of those with addictions is a lack of a romantic interest. Honestly. He has no history of epilepsy and is taking no medications from a doctor for 'psychological problems'. Now let's dive in...

4. *Q: What are the problems you want to solve today?* A: 'I want to stop taking cocaine. (Unequivocal.) I also gamble too much.' (RH: I decide to tackle

cocaine only; my reasoning will become clear later...)

5. *Q: When did this begin? Was there a triggering event?* A: 'I was young, I did it with (BLEEP! relatives); I smoked cannabis first. I had fun and had a good time – and then **it got a hold of me*.** I ignored it for quite a while.' So a pretty typical entry point into drugs – marijuana is a gateway drug. (*Note the kinaesthetic languaging – 'hold'!)

6. *Q: How often do you use cocaine?* A: '3-4 times a week. I lack the willpower to stop.' Drug abuse is almost NEVER predominantly about willpower; that's just what people are conditioned to say. What they mean by 'willpower' is a whole host of factors they are unaware of.

7. *Q: How often do you enjoy it?* A: 'I don't; I hate it – I keep running out and having to get more.' He has lost control.

8. *Q: Would you describe drug/habit X etc. as your friend? What does it do for you? What's the purpose or intention you have while taking it?* A: 'It's not a friend at all. It's an enemy! I feel compelled to do it.' The subconscious has taken over.

9. *Q: On a scale of 0-10, 0 being **no desire*** (first covert embed – he is emotional, seeking help and so suggestible already) *to stop and 10 being 100% motivated; how would you honestly rate your true **desire to stop** doing X?* A: '10! I've had enough!' I believe him – he says this emphatically. The 'enough is enough' point has been reached. His life is crap – he *longs* for change.

10. *Q: What are the list of reasons you want to stop X?* A: 'Financially. All my money goes to the drug dealers. It masters me. I am losing my family and friends. I don't go to work. I binge and isolate myself. I have panic attacks after taking the coke and end up in A and E (Accident and Emergency – equivalent to ER is US). They give me EEGs and everything...etc.' He has got himself in one big hole. He is ashamed and desperately wants to dig himself out. I can help him.

11. *Q: What things have you done to overcome this and how successful were they?* A: 'I go to CA, Cocaine Anonymous (RH note: in my opinion a quasi-mind control 'cult' like AA – see later section). I have relapsed* a couple

of times (I'll say!)' He says something about 'obsessions lifting'. I talk to him about CA etc., how it operates and why their 'approach' is doomed. I tell him to stop going to the 'meetings'. (*The concept of 'relapse' will be dealt with later.)

12. *Q: What do you enjoy most about life?* A: 'Spending time with friends. Doing normal things.'

13. *Q: In what situations do you feel most happy, secure and confident?* A: 'I use cocaine so much. It's so extreme. I get a feeling but...I feel ashamed. I feel guilty.' RH: I fucking hate drugs – anyone who sells them is scum. Anyone who promotes them as healthy is an idiotic and dangerous dog turd. You should see the human remains at my end asshole! Poor bastard – imagine this was your life!

14. *Q: What achievements are you most proud of?* A: He tells me about the usual things – job qualifications in the construction industry, passing his driving test etc. This is a man who has a great potential to be happy. Why? His goals are very modest. He is not an incredibly ambitious person. He tells me that his life has been 'massively put on hold'. He

wants to do all the conventional things the culture and TV have hypnotised him to desire – he wants to 'go travelling', especially to Thailand (the hookers!?). He wants to climb a mountain etc. – this is the first inkling that this man is not taking enough risks - as I have written about in other books, if men do not take enough risks, for whatever reason, they can sink into addiction.

15. *Q: What strengths do have that will help you* ***overcome this problem****?* (Throwing in these embeds is wholly unneeded but you can, if you wish.) A: 'I can't maintain my willpower for any length. I need to say no. I need to be strong.' Actually his problem is not based on a lack of any of these things. He is not getting his needs met. This makes him unhappy. He also has an automatic habit loop in his unconscious we call an 'addiction'. People with no understanding of the mind, including family members, often see addiction as some kind of character defect. It isn't. It is a natural response to stress.

16. *Q: If you could rate your self-worth from 0-10, 10 being* ***you feel great about yourself*** *and 0 utterly worthless, what would it be?* A: 'Now?

It's on the floor! 3 out of 10. I feel worthless. I take stupid risks; I gamble (more of this in session 2).' If a client has 'situational low-self-esteem/worth', which I define as a temporary low self-evaluation brought on by the presenting problem etc. then I do not 'fix it'. I find it 'gets better' spontaneously when the addiction etc. is hypnotically negotiated away. If the value a person gives themselves was low before the drug taking, I fix it. Low self-worth makes people feel crap, when they feel crap they take drugs: quite simple really.

17. *Q: Do you exercise?* A: 'No.' I go into my 'it's good to exercise' spiel. See 'Powerful hypnosis' for details.

18. *Q: Do you have any intuitive sense of what has to change within yourself to get the desired change?* A: 'Feelings! I need to feel good. My good feelings are all gone.' ***Drug addiction, food addiction, all addictions are ALL about feelings!*** If natural good feelings are present, guess what? People generally don't become addicted.

19. *Q: Can you think of an image, metaphor or symbol that represents either the problem or solution that you want etc.?* A: 'A poison bottle and the

solution would be the sun and trees and freedom.' ***Hint for therapists: use this in the hypnosis phase – he has given you his personal symbology!*** I'll show you how after the following script. Natural world imagery is often neurologically linked to good feeling states. In the appendix I use a deepener to create a nice stroll through nature – it makes people feel good naturally. Artificiality = human misery. Naturalness = human happiness and health.

20. *Q: Is there any reason you shouldn't* change? *Are there any parts that don't want to? Do you have warring parts?* A: 'No, I just want this done without any other help.'

21. *Q: What has prevented the change you want up till now?* A: 'No idea!' That's why they come to see us therapists; they assume we know!

22. *Q: Have you ever made a similar change or reached a point in your life where you thought, 'I've had enough and I'm moving forward in a more positive direction?'* A: 'Yes quite a lot of times.'

NFH: you get rapport naturally by asking

JUST the right questions.

In essence that was the interview. He understood what hypnosis was during our pre-talk and was happy for me to hypnotise him. Without further ado...

RH's crushing cocaine addiction script.
Step 1: Dissociate client from taking x – cocaine.

(Deep hypnosis assumed)

'As you rest in this place of healing...recall a time when you felt the urge to use cocaine, in the past...Be in that time fully *(associated frame)*...That's it. I don' t know what you were doing or who you were with – you do. As you feel that old feeling you got when you felt you had wanted that stuff...notice how that old process had negatively hypnotised and entranced you...You once had choice and freedom and then 'snap'!: before you knew it you were dependent. Something had taken over your brain and its subconscious processes –

The good thing is we can ***stop that process now...*** You felt compelled, out of control – BUT...Float out of that time right now...ensuring ***you have sufficient distance from that habit...*** And see that you over there who used to use that garbage that's been ruining your life up until now...***Look at that old you*** ***objectively...***

Notice everything you can about that former situation...That you was hypnotised by that stuff...That brain was dependent and hooked... That person was clearly not in control of their mind...As you look at that rather pitiful scene know, really know at the deepest levels of who you are that ***'Enough is enough!'*** Resolve now that it really is exactly the right time to ***make some very profound changes unconsciously, now...***

You are beginning to ***dissociate from that hypnotic additive mind-set...***All parts of you are finding very real ways to ***become free from those old mental processes*** that held you back – that had entranced you previously... Somehow from the most hopeful parts of yourself you ***feel a deep determination*** rising from the wellsprings of who you REALLY are...

Okay! Pick another time when you felt compelled to use coke/marijuana etc. Be in that time and place – doing whatever you did. Anyone would think – ***you're sick of that.*** That dictating urge from that parasitically poisonous white powder *(etc.)* that's been holding you back for far too long...Robbing you of a real chance to ***get your genuine emotional needs satisfied...Now...***maybe the last jaded high that wasn't that good anyway, when you really examine it...And the good thing is ***that old pattern can change...***

Again – float right out of that time so that ***you have fully dissociated from those old habits and addictive mind-set*** – you ***left it in the past, now...***Look at that you who was being bullied, robbed, conned! Would you let a person dictate to you like that? That person over there was trapped – negatively entranced by that drug...See them as they are...What has it done to them physically – inside and out?

It's ***time to stand up to it...****Is that person a slave? Or do they want to* ***be totally free of that former process, now...***Isn't it time to ***make genuine, new choices...*** (?)
What truths about that person can you see when ***you are objectively detached from that response...***Does the situation teach you anything important?

You'll ***find certain associations are changing*** at a deep level...as a result of this changing process. What if you could know, really know that...a person's focus can change...
You can ***reconnect to natural pleasures...***
The ones you were born with; hardwired to experience...Was the old experience really that good? Behaving in those ways that you did?
Is that what you truly wanted for yourself?

One last time for luck – ***choose*** another time when you were being bullied and dictated to by that drug...Aren't you just sick and tired of its old fishwife nagging? Who is ***in control, here*** (?) Isn't it just boring? A waste of life time and your hard earned cash that you gave to that parasitic drug and dealer – isn't it time to ***sensibly rebel!***

One last time: feel that old, boring time and that hypnotically compelling feeling to endanger yourself like that, playing Russian roulette with your life...Were you really caring about yourself or those you love? Don't ***you deserve more than that*** (?) Better ways are possible...

And just as you felt that impulse to smoke it or snort it...***float far away from that old unwanted response...***As you view that time objectively...what specifically about that time ***displeases you*** most? What damage has it done or might it do? I know you ***care deeply and want to change fundamentally once and for all...***Wouldn't it be good to ***feel absolutely NO desire! Now!*** When – for the last time, you look at that person...Look at what their life had come to. Did the innocent child full of promise deserve all that crap? Is that what their life was all about? Is short term pseudo-satisfaction going to work anymore? Did it ever, really? Each and both of you know the answers...The good thing is you came here fully motivated to ***alter certain responses... perceptions...attitudes...ideas and feelings!*** And the deeper self will assist you in this ***healthy desire only now...***

So now you have done that...Now, that ***your brain is relaxed and capable of reflecting calmly on reality...***we can start the process of ***you're building in such good feelings and more positive responses*** without knowing how consciously...These learnings are imprinting and embedding in those places they need to...Certain mechanisms facilitate this.

Step 2: Associating into positive responses.

When you were born, you were born with such wonderful potential...You knew instinctively how to ***have healthy fun...***You knew how to ***derive joy from living and play...***This world enchanted you, as a child...*('as a child' is an indirect command for age regression to occur...)* You knew how to laugh and that was free...You knew how to talk to friends and relatives that you loved...You knew how to do all those creative things you did...You had a natural innocence and curiosity to ***learn so many things...***Textures that pleased you... Spontaneity! Tastes and sounds...You'll find it helps to ***adopt a position in life that helps you lighten up*** about so many things...Sights and smells...***Having the wisdom*** of a child to do that which helps you ***gain mastery...*** over so many differing things...The way each blade of grass is differently green...The way the light is...at different times of day and the changing seasons...The clouds and the sky are always beautifully unique and changing...The wind in the tress...The sun on your skin...The delicious joy of an ice cream...The **bliss you feel** on holidays/vacations...Can you remember running just to ***feel the joy*** of doing it?

As a child ***physically you repair easily, now...***How you couldn't stop a laugh! How you wanted to sing! Dance! Make things! Go places that were new! Meet interesting people! The joyous way your body and mind felt being used for natural joys! ***Deep layers of bliss lay within you! Reconnect to them, now...***Just remembering is joyful! That's right! See what you saw! Hear what you heard! Feel what you felt! Deeply...

As a result of this changing process ***your thoughts, feeling and perspectives have reframed and shifted for the better...*** And that's a truly nice thing to know, is it not? You ***feel an inner resolve and firm determination*** unlike anything you have ever known to...***completely break free, reclaim your life, now!!!*** You have ancient, instinctive pathways deep in the neurology bequeathed you by your toughest ancestors to ***enjoy life***

naturally everyday...to ***get any missing needs met safely, happily, realistically...*** You never lost any of that heritage...You have the power to ***re-associate to your power...*** To ***heal.*** To know. To ***change.*** To ***mature.*** To ***outgrow.*** To ***go beyond.*** To ***find new fulfilling ways.*** To ***know intimacy.*** To ***know connection.*** To ***know love.*** To ***laugh.*** To ***feel joyous!*** To ***smile, deep inside*** in recognition that you know the happiness of being with significant others and just talking...You can become absorbed by so many things that truly interest and engage your mind, body and soul... Won't it be wonderful discovering what that will be like?

Now, you really are somebody who has unique needs that need fulfilment...Take some time to consider that while I'm quiet...*(pause 15-30 seconds...)*

Good! That's right. You really have a body that needs good food, fresh air and exercise - Take some time to consider that while I'm quiet... *(pause 15-30 seconds...)*

That's it: ***take care of it sensibly...***You can feel a deep connection to your interests and to ***stimulating that mind healthily and positively from now on...***Take some time to consider that while I'm quiet...*(pause 15-30 seconds...)*

Excellent! We all need challenge, accomplishment, respect; the ability to ***have fun, relax and rest too...***You ***feel so much calmer*** knowing this is so.

Step 3: Getting the brain to adjust to withdrawal.

Isn't a bit of temporary irritation...not always 100% at your best perhaps or not...really such a short space of time...a very small price worth paying, is it not? Actions have consequences... That great brain of yours knows how to adjust at just the right pace, in the right way, as it detoxifies and works properly ***without artificial assistance*** again. Day by day, moment by passing moment, you ***feel so much better within yourself...***That time seems to pass so very quickly...Confident people can handle all of the problems in life that need solving...We need problems, they're interesting, solvable. They help us ***gain strength when you overcome any adversity...***It's time for more interesting, joy-soaked problems...Ones that genuinely stimulate all of who you are! Sooner than you know ***things just settle and work properly...***There can be great ***comfort inside*** these understandings...You have unlearned what you had learned, wasn't it?

Step 4: Future pace – mental rehearsal of total success.

Dissociated practise.

Like watching a fascinating film...imagine now a freely confident future you who is ***over that...*** Having moved beyond what you weren't really anyway...You can even look back and laugh... Jokes are often founded on past errors...See yourself in a situation that will 100% confirm for you that this has worked! You are ***acting differently...***You ***have choice...***If you are in a certain place or with people who offer that which you don't want...you are able to ***decline comfortably and confidently, now...***in your own words and way...Others make their own choices, they really do, and you do likewise... Maybe you feel a bit sorry for them?

Associated future experience.

When ***you are happy*** with that scene...float inside that flexible, powerful, confident you and go through that experience from the beginning from the inside...See through those drug free eyes! Hear through those ears that ***hear the right messages, only...***Feel how confident, relaxed and open you are to so many new experiences, people, places...What will you do with all your free time? *(Allow a full minute or so!)*

Great. It's funny when we look back on things from a certain objective distance of time and what once seemed so important is ***just a faded memory of what was...***You can ***feel that way now.*** Your future looks so good. You ***make it so!*** An abundance of ***good feelings within...***You ***feel more strength, assuredness and certainty*** than you have ever known tha-at...***things have changed permanently, for the better, now.*** And that's a nice thing to know, haven't you?

(All the change has been rehearsed – the brain has re-associated and knows what to do – it has a template. Now we ratify the change at deep levels, assuring no warring parts, through a hypnotic negotiation process; the most important stage in the addiction deprogramming process. Did I mention that already??! ;)

Part 2: Advanced parts negotiation procedure variant 2.

(NFH: I use this phase in all addiction stopping first sessions. It is my opinion and experience that the specific negotiation procedure that follows is the key to success in 99% of the sessions I do. It can be used or modified for a whole host of problems – in 'Powerful hypnosis' I gave a variant of it to halt unexplained 'psychosomatic' pain. I have used it for weight

loss too: it is immensely powerful. I prefer it to the one I showed you in the stop smoking permanently script. Again: when I speak to parts in drug addiction work I never ask for ideomotor confirmation of subconscious agreement: I assume it and move on confidently. Imagine you are offering an intelligent but cheeky child the choice of going to bed now or going to bed now! Just do it in a really nice and pleasant way.

Any condescension or 'judge-mentalism' at any point will ruin everything!!! I always aim to get success in one session: at least major and significant progress. You should too. The client almost always appreciates the effort, even if the method is somewhat bizarre!!! Hypnosis IS bizarre!)

We are now going to carry out a process of negotiation with all the parts of mind: the functions, if you will, that with the best of intentions maintained that past habit...

1. **Create a 'place of agreement'.** Just imagine a place in your mind where only agreement is possible, now...That great. I don't know what that place looks like...It's totally unique to you...Trust exactly what the subconscious offers in response to my words, ideas, suggestions. *(5-7 secs pause.)*

2. **Create some sort of seating arrangement.** As you ***rest and relax even deeper...***I think it would be a good idea to imagine some things that can be sat on – whatever you want...Enough for 8 parts that will help you ***succeed in your own way...***which will soon be called upon to assist...in fact they are ready and expecting us...

3. **Create a 'place of honour/authority'.** And you need a place to sit yourself that indicates that YOU are in charge of this process...So if you haven't already, take a seat in the 'place of honour/authority' please...*(Pause a beat.)* Good.

4. **Conditioning with pleasure protocol (optional).** Before we move on, I just want to say something – making a positive change makes ***you feel good.*** Good feelings, it is known, make positive, creative change easier. With that in mind... whenever we reach full agreement with a part, the subconscious mind can allow you to ***experience any wonderful feeling*** that it feels would best suit the occasion. After we have concluded a stage in this process I will click my fingers and say 'reward' and you will feel an amazing feeling instantly! And that's nice to know isn't it? *(Create motivation to change with*

'pleasure rewards' that are natural and reteach the brain that it can make the person feel good for no good reason at all in one go! Also you will notice I add in the use of 'colour feeling' intensifiers to boost any good feelings elicited in this process – see book 1 and 2 for a full description.)

5. **Contact habit x maintenance part (originator).** Now we can begin...Can you simply invite the part of you that made you use x *(cocaine etc.)* to this agreeable place. Just watch as they take a seat. However your subconscious represents that part is just right for you instinctively – just trust it.

6. **Part that started and maintained unwanted habit (the originator/maintainer) let's the client know its intention.** Okay. Now that part that used to make them use/abuse x in the past: please can you let this person know your positive intent in making them do so back then. I'll be quiet for a bit while you do just that. *(Pause for 10 secs.)*

7. **Negotiate with 'originator'/'maintainer'/behaviour maintenance part.** Great. Thanks for that. The fact is this person now deeply desires to **be free of x/cocaine etc.** Whatever the original intent was, whatever

you once thought, they have found out that that intent is fine but the behaviour that attempted to satisfy that is very unhealthy. And it doesn't work. Where you once thought and felt one thing – they know think and feel a whole new set of things. This individual has their own reasons why they want to ***change habits*** – they told me all about them; and there might even be more: and I know you know better than me what they are. You will gain a new role in their life; it's better, more functional and genuinely satisfying. Will you now agree to ***stop making them do x/cocaine*** etc. and ***be free of that,*** so that they/he/she etc. live longer, more healthily and happily than ever before? Can you ***do that*** for them? *(Pause for 10 seconds or so – in hyper-responsive clients they'll smile and nod; it's very funny and charming to watch! If you see no response, assume the part has agreed and move on. I have NEVER had it refuse.) (Click fingers)*...And 'REWARD!' That's it!!! ...***Feel really good*** about this, in your own way. *(Let them bathe in that state a bit...)* Now take that feeling and turn it into a colour and let it spread all throughout your mind and body feeling better... better...even better! That's it! That wonderful feeling intensifies deep inside!

8. **Contact 'gifted/innovative/creative part'.** Excellent! Thanks for that. Now, can you please invite the wonderful creative part of you that some call 'the creative unconscious' to this place? This is the part that generates all your ideas, those solutions, fuels and guides your powerful imagination, it creates dreams at night time, it is one of the most important parts of you in fact. It solves problems while you sleep and the answers pop into your mind as insights, intuitions and feelings; you know the kind of thing. It does these things in many ways – it really does and always will only better. I'll just be quiet while you do that and as they take a seat somewhere appropriate. *(Pause 10 secs or so.)*

9. **Ask creative part to generate multiple new choices unconsciously.** Very good. Now creative part/creative unconscious of this person: as you know, the part that made them use x has already agreed that they will now help them ***stop that behaviour once and for all, now.*** But in order to ***succeed*** they will need something to replace that former drug using/excessive drinking/overeating etc. activity that will provide as good as if not a better outcome than that old unwanted habit provided. As we carry on with this

healing process in this place, can you simply ***come up with some alternative activities*** that they could choose from to replace the old unhealthy habit? Can you work on that while we proceed and we'll get back to you soon? *(Pause a beat or so only)* Good. *(Click fingers)*...And 'REWARD!' That's right! ***Feel amazing*** somehow about this. *(Let them bathe in that state a bit...)* Now take that feeling and turn it into a colour and let it spread all throughout your mind and body feeling better...better... even better! That's it! That wonderful feeling intensifies deep inside!

10. **Contact 'stubborn/tenacious/relentless part'.** Now – what we need is the help of the steadfast/stubborn part of you. This part is very powerful and knowledgeable – it is very ***self-willed indeed.*** It actually controls what you will do and won't do. It knows your deepest values and true conscience; it protects you from unwanted influence. It also guides your best decisions. If it has to it will firmly, relentlessly stand its ground to enforce its lists of dos and don'ts! It has principles. Its own code of ethics if you will. It does it brilliantly and always has. Can you invite them here please and watch as they take just the right place in this process while

I'm quiet for a bit? *(Pause for 5-10 secs.)*

11. **<u>Negotiate with ornery, headstrong/inflexible/stubborn part.</u>** Perfect. Now stubborn/steadfast part of this person – I know you keep the lists of what they will do and what they won't. As this person truly and deeply desires to ***be free of that old habit*** that has held them back in so many ways as you well know; can you ***take that past activity off of that list*** of what they will do and just ***put it on the list of things they definitely won't anymore*** and use your great capacities to properly ***enforce that change*** (?) Can you please ***agree*** to do that for all the appropriate reasons? *(Pause 10 secs.) (Click fingers)*...And 'REWARD!' That's it! ***Feel something really good*** about this. Your mind knows how to make ***you feel good naturally!*** *(Let them bathe in that state a bit...)* Now take that feeling and turn it into a colour and let it spread all throughout your mind and body feeling better... better...even better! That's it! That wonderful feeling intensifies deep inside!

12. **<u>Contact the 'mutinous/insurgent/defiant/rebel part'</u>**. *(The reason you contact the 'rebel'/'independence' part is twofold: 1.*

All drug takers are cultural conformists and not rebels at all. Never let them know this! They perceive that taking drugs is cool, rebellious etc.; mainly through media and peer group programming – I call this 'rebel part hijacking'. The fact is the rebel part is a bit of a twit. He is a rebel without a cause, more a curse!!! 2. The rebel part can rebel against the therapist/hypnotist - so if you 'co-opt the rebel', one of the oldest military/political strategies known to man you neutralise it: it is now your ally. Bingo!) Now there is a part of you that is very brave and independent minded if you like. It is always looking out for your best interests *(flatter it!)*. It is always reaching out for ***your total independence.*** It has never liked, on occasion hated being controlled, bullied or told what it should and shouldn't do by others and rightly so – it wants you to have autonomy/independence, self-reliance, freedom and more besides. It doesn't like being forced to do something by someone or something else either – like x *(habit)* has been doing lately to you. Can you invite what I call your rebel part and just watch as he/she takes a necessary and vital place in this changing process. *(Pause a beat etc.)*

13. <u>**Negotiate with the 'defiant one'/rebel *etc.***</u> Thanks. Now rebel part of this person. I know your role in their life. I want to thank you for that. You know this person deeply desires to ***stop doing coke etc.*** As this is the case now, can you please ***give your full support to this team*** by reminding this person, unconsciously if you like, that <u>*they*</u> are making this needed change because it's what <u>*they*</u> truly, deeply want to do at this point in their lives. They are doing it because it is what <u>*they*</u> desire. Not because me or anyone else is trying to make them do anything. I cannot make anyone do anything because this part would ***stand up to tyrannical behaviour*** and rightly so. There's a time to ***defy certain orders in radical ways.*** No one is trying to make them ***do it*** – it's their own decision to ***complete this process of change, now.*** The thing is it's really time to ***rebel from that drug/habit/tyranny*** etc., is it not? And so you need a new role too - can you ***help this person change,*** in the best and most appropriate ways, and remind them of their great reasons for doing so if necessary? Will you agree to do that now? *(Pause for 5 -7 secs etc.)* Great that is fantastic – you are doing really well! *(Click fingers)*...And 'REWARD!' That's it! ***Feel***

really good about this process ***now.*** The way you process certain information is already changing, unconsciously, positively, now...*(Let them bathe in that state a bit...)* Now take that feeling and turn it into a colour and let it spread all throughout your mind and body feeling better... better... even better! That's it! That wonderful feeling intensifies deep inside!

14. **Older/wiser/objective adult you tutors younger you.** I simply want you to recall the very first time you used that drug etc. Locate that memory. That's it. Now, can the adult you let that younger you know with common sense, in unequivocal terms - clearly and with a sense of certainty I might add, as you might kindly advise your own child, how bad, really bad the idea of starting with that old behaviour really was because no one knows better than that part *(which part? Ambiguous/confusing)*. It can be nice at any age to ***hear/here wise advice.*** Remember always, ultimately ***you want the same things,*** is that not so? Again I'll be quiet while you do that. *(Pause for 10-15 seconds to let them chat/communicate etc.)*

15. **<u>Negotiate with 'naïve self' and offer a new role.</u>** Great. Can you invite that part to this place and let them sit down. *(Pause a beat.)* Okay – younger you, sometimes we need to hear the truth like it or not: that's reality. I would like you to play a new role in this person's life. You know how much they deeply desire to ***be free of that old habit forever.*** The wiser you has made it crystal clear how much they want this. In order for them to ***be fully successful*** we need you to do something more rewarding – whenever this person even so much as ponders or thinks about using x *(coke)* again, can you agree to give them that same sort of wakeup call that you just received? Give them the advice and guidance you just got – in blunt terms they will understand about how bad, foolish, dangerous and unhealthy an idea like that would be. How it would be a big step in the wrong direction. Can you agree to ***take on this new role*** please? *(Pause for 5-7 secs.)* Great. It's amazing how well you are doing. *(Click fingers)*...And 'REWARD!' That's it! Feel really good about this process now. The way you do certain things is already changing, at the deepest levels of experience, now... *(Let them bathe in that state a bit...)* Now take that feeling and turn it into a colour and let it spread all throughout your mind and body

feeling better...better...even better! That's it! That wonderful feeling intensifies deep inside!

16. **Invite the 'inner strength' part to the process.** *(Ego State Therapy rightly identifies a part called 'inner strength'. This is the strong, leadership part of us. It is the bit that gets you through the tough times etc.)* Excellent! Can you now invite the strongest part of who you truly are – some people call this part 'inner strength', the strong part, the powerful part, the leadership part. It is the toughest, strongest, most no-nonsense part of who you are. It provides you with ***inner strength whenever you need it, now;*** every team needs a leader. There may be future times where and when a part of you needs the support of your strength and inner resolve to ***succeed.*** I want inner strength to agree now to take on this always strongly supportive role when required so that ***this person can achieve that goal*** – do you agree to help? *(Pause for 5-7 secs.)* Great. You are doing really well. *(Click fingers)*...And 'REWARD!' That's it! Feel really good about this process now. The way you do certain things is already changing, at the deepest levels of experience, now...*(Let them bathe in that state a bit...)* Now take that

feeling and turn it into a colour and let it spread all throughout your mind and body feeling better...better...even better! That's it! That wonderful feeling intensifies deep inside! *(In waking life, chains of good feeling DO indicate we are moving forward successfully – this is a hypnotic sped-up version of this process. Note: some therapists have claimed that the neocortex = the strong part. We need more than a neocortex to 'be strong'; the whole mind needs to be involved – these 'parts' are metaphors: do not be too concrete!)*

17. **Asking the innovator to provide new resources + all parts in agreement on the best one/ones.** Okay now gifted/creative part, I asked if you could generate some healthy alternative activities that this person could do instead of using cocaine/chocolate binges etc. that will supply them with at least as good as, if not a much more satisfying outcome that x did. What specifically are they? Can all parts now discuss and agree upon which activity or activities if you prefer will be the main replacement for the old drug/habit/etc. use. The answer must be unanimous. Can all parts now agree to ***help them do these new sets of behaviours and resources*** when required instead of that past activity for so

many obvious reasons? (*Wait 10-15 secs.) (Click fingers)*...And 'REWARD!' That's it! Feel really good about this process now. Make this the best state so far! The way you do many certain things is profoundly changing, at the deepest levels of experience, now...*(Let them bathe in that state a bit...)* Now take that feeling and turn it into a colour and let it spread all throughout your mind and body feeling better...better...even better! That's it! That wonderful feeling intensifies deep inside! *(Good doggies get a reward!)*

18. Good. And finally...steadfast part, will you place this activity or these activities on the list of things they definitely will do in place of that old ***x/cocaine use*** that you ***removed from that list.*** *(Covert run on – 'x use removed from that list'* subliminal/strobonic injection). Can you ***do that now please*** (?) Excellent – you are doing so well! And one last time for luck - (Click fingers)...And 'REWARD!' That's it! The best pleasure state ever now! Feel really good about this process. Make this the best state so far! *This change is necessary and the necessary is always possible, noooo-oooow!** *(Let them bathe in that state a bit...)* Now take that feeling and turn it into a colour and let it spread all throughout your mind and body feeling

better...better...even better! That's it! That wonderful feeling intensifies deep inside! Keep an appropriate level of all these good feelings. *(*This is a 'super-suggestion': feel free to use it with any other change work you may do!)*

Part 3: Symbology re-association work - cutting old connections away.

2 more quick things to do to ***wrap this up fully.*** First...

1. **Identify symbolic connections to habit x.** Notice something that you hadn't noticed before...There is a table before you somewhere in this place...on top of it are 8 ultra-sharp blades that will slice through anything, even steel. There are 8 pairs of night vision goggles too. Each part, please take a knife and place the cool looking night vision goggles on your head. *(Pause for 5-7 secs.)* Good. Switch the night goggles on by flicking a switch on them. Okay. Suddenly the lights go out. There is total and utter darkness. But you can still sense all that is around you perfectly somehow – like a 6th sense. You ***feel safe and in control.*** But you can notice here and there bright green cables/threads/chains – some imaginative representation of the old cords, the old

bindings that connected you to all the old triggers that you associated with doing x – they might symbolise people, places, states of mind and body: you don't need to know exactly; just get a sense of that because your unconscious knows precisely what I mean. Because once upon a time you had bought or wrought your own chains and now it's time, really time to ***break all those old chains*** that held you back. Okay, in order to ***move forward in this process*** you must, once and for all, ***cut those old connections completely, now.*** On my cue...use those knives that slice those old associations, triggers, connections that held you back like a hot knife through butter so easily! In a moment, not now but in a moment I will click my fingers/say 'Go!' etc. and you can, as a team, slice all those chains/connections etc. so very quickly and thoroughly so that they are all gone. It only takes a few seconds in trance. Okay. You ready? *(Rhetorical.)* And...*(CLICK FINGERS! Fart etc. Pause for 5-10 secs)* Very good.

2. **Locate and destroy hidden associations to x.** Next, there is a dial on the side of your night goggles – turn it clockwise all of you and this will reveal something unexpected – all the secret,

hidden connections to that old habit are now revealed. It order to ***ditch that habit permanently*** you must cut those too. On my cue please ***finish the job*** and remove any old associations to that former behaviour, now...*(CLICK FINGERS etc.! Pause 5 secs or so...)* And that is that. I would like to thank all the parts of you for helping out. They can all now get back to their new functions, unconsciously on your behalf, now. That's right. You can thank them too. Perfect! As a result you ***feel deeply congruent.***

Part 4: Reaching a crossroads in life symbology.

We have all had times in our lives when we ***cross a threshold into a new, improved phase of living.*** It's like you enter some paths in life that you just know will be life changingly beneficial to you and ***you just know this.*** And this is such a time in the great adventure and journey that is your life: you have chosen to ***move toward health, now,*** that is a great path to take. Your new healthier attitudes will benefit you in so many ways.

In order to ***solidify this change*** I want you to imagine you are in a land that symbolically represents that old habit. It might be a dingy, dirty place; a place you have outgrown now. It might look ugly in some way, unnatural. I don't know what that place is like – you do. But the good thing is, as you look ahead you can see a brighter place not too far ahead – instinctively you know, really know that this is your final destination in this healing process. You know it and **want it.** Feel the joyous anticipation of that healthier way of life that is symbolised by that place ahead of you – you get closer and closer. It might be a beautiful place of serenity and peace – it may be pretty, sunny, it could be a particular place in nature. It's good to ***get in touch with natural living.***

As you walk confidently towards that place, a beautiful bubble floats toward you and stops just before you...That's it! It is quite large and you can see your reflection in it! You look radiantly healthy. In order to go to the new place in a purified way you must ***get rid of any remaining junk that you used to associate with that old habit*** – get a sense now of some colour that symbolises any remaining crap, doubts, fears, past attitudes, anything you need to let go of; maybe it's the stuff you used to use the drug and imagine it going into that bubble, purifying you for your new way of life that lies just ahead. I'll be quiet while you do that. *(Wait about 10 secs.)* Good. Now that bubble floats off and ***you feel purified deep within.***

There is a place, a dividing line where the old

place ends and the new place begins. In order to ***be drug free for life*** you need to cross that boundary marker from one way of less than living, to living your life with zest! You reach that line now and in a moment, soon, you will cross that line and it will ***feel amazing.*** Are you ready? Once you cross that divide there is no going back: you live your life as a person who is fully healthy and free. ***Free of that junk, now.*** Okay! GO FOR IT! Cross into that new place with 100% commitment to ***remain steadfast in your decision.***

Excellent – and now...an incredible feeling washes through you making you ***feel glad to be alive*** and to be you living this amazing gift of life. A life of more positive relationships, the air seems fresher and more pure, like mountain air here! The sky is beautiful! The sights and sounds of nature seem positively enhanced and intensified in almost magical ways! There are more interesting challenges here. Realistic goals seem totally achievable! You ***feel rooted, confident and free!*** Feel that sense of freedom. Take a last look behind you at that old unattractive, repellent, dingy place. As you do, ***your resolve only grows.*** Take some time now to look around you at the better place you have entered – feel how good you feel. You are in control now. I'll be quiet while you explore and ponder things in this place, things that are meaningful and relevant to your healing process. *(Quiet for a full 20 secs.)*

Great! Last thing to do: imagine being in a situation that will confirm ***this has worked*** – say 12 months from now. You are a healthy individual, so much happier, a good person, lighter inside, smiling more – getting your needs met naturally, listening to the wisdom of emotions, intuitions, insights that bubble up now and a-gain from your deeper mind. This new person that you always were ***deep, deep inside*** has been reconnected to.

As you imagine going through that situation feeling so strong and confident, assured and knowing you can handle anything that arises your unconscious finalises any and all re-organisations, re-associations and anything else that needs to occur so that ***you live your life healthily*** from now on. Changing only in the ways that are safest right now. And that's a nice thing to be sure about, is it not?

And you can ***get that knowing feeling*** that this work is complete: you are certain in that place where that sense of certainty resides, now. And every time ***you stick to this decision*** it reinforces that decision and your unconscious releases a genuine feeling of pride in your continuing accomplishment.

And now I'll begin the waking up process - you

did brilliantly! Well done etc...'

(You could add in some summation suggestions but that ought to do the trick – add in a withdrawal coping model – see appendix and begin the wake up or exduction protocol you're most comfortable with. You can do this confidently Padawan: this stuff works powerfully!)

Extra note: using the client's symbolism.

If you remember the interview phase, our imaginary client said cocaine = a phial of poison, and health = sun and trees etc. At some point in the change work phase you can incorporate this imagery. For example,

'You can see a small bottle of poison on a table. Go over to it and using the pair of safety gloves pick it up and put it into an industrial waste disposal unit. That's it. Get rid of that junk! Turn on the unit and know that that poison is gone from your life. Perfect! This acts as a sign and a signal that ***you are free once more.*** *The fact is your haven't lost anything – you now* ***own health!***

Now look over there – passed the table and waste disposal zone is the 'free you zone' – it is glorious, exciting here, the sun shines through the trees: it looks like a place in a legend or

fairy story, but it is very real and lifelike to you: go to that place now, knowing that as you do, you ***leave the unwanted in the past because you intend to ACT DIFFERENTLY, now!'***

I usually just ad-lib this stuff from what clients tell me. It's a pretty easy process to incorporate. The underlying principles I hope are obvious.

Analysis of process.

- In the first stage I do what I always do – **dissociate a person from habit/state x** hypnotically. I then **associate them into a healthier future** and lob in some helpful suggestions to support the change – good feelings, re-associations etc. But that isn't enough.

- **Naming parts:** I often use terms like 'Innovator' or 'Gifted' etc. part where others say 'creative' or use more mundane language. Why? Because they sound more dynamic, inspiring and exciting: this makes the process of change more attractive! There needs to be more 'show biz' in therapeutic hypnosis – your clients want magic! Give it to them.

- In the second stage I negotiate fully with all relevant parts that maintain a problem. ***I offer them better ways – NEVER KILL OFF A PART: you change its specific outcome (druggie behaviour etc.) NOT its underlying function.*** Imagine saying: sure you have £/$5; would you like a million instead? Who's gonna say no?! Exactly. Sometimes you'll know the person has changed the behaviour because they'll wake up and say – 'I need to exercise!' That's the feedback. Sometimes they just can't stop smiling; some are miserable bastards and just sort of huff in some way, as if to say, 'Good. That worked.'

- While I used the bubble to remove niggling doubts etc. you can use anything that symbolises their removal. Easy – study the underlying principles of the things I have shown you in this book and invent your own stuff, please do improve on mine. After all YOU are the healer.

- ***Note: when adapted these negotiation formulas can be used in real world negotiations too.***

That was session one: our friend the former coke head is free of coke, for 3 months, he never wants to go back. His life is better *experientially.* It's just that his gambling habit is a bit of a nuisance: In fact it's a bit worse. Don't panic. It happens – it's a stage in the healing process. Let's deal with that next...

Remember: a problem matrix is sometimes a complex thing – take down the most prominent obstacle first. You demolish its other support structures in your second attack blitz – always remembering to offer better solutions.

Session 2: Gambling addiction removal.

'And the cat came back the very next day...'
'I think you are some kind of miracle worker,' he said to me.
'That's kind but the reality is YOU did the work, I just guided you through the process.' (I never accept that I have some unique healing powers etc.: I really, really don't! I just genuinely know how the brain works to a higher degree than most people.)

Let's get on with session two, the final interview and intervention with the former Cocaine Kid. We get the social pleasantries out the way – I always get down to business; I am not their friend – they aren't mine: if client's talk too much I just look at them, remain quiet and smile as if to say, 'That's nice. Shall we get on with it?' I am not an Agony Uncle!

Interview 2: Gambling addiction and self-belief/self-acceptance boost.

1. *Q: Okay, tell me what has happened since the last session?* A: 'I have been 3 ½ months clean.'

2. *Q: Tell me about the gambling addiction – how does it manifest itself?* A: 'I haven't got any money so I go into the bookies; there is not one happy person in there. I do not enjoy going in there, but it's a compulsion. It's the *feeling** I get after I've laid the bet.' (*Again – drugs/addiction processes are about FEELINGS!!!)

3. *Q: How long has gambling been a problem?* A: 'I have almost always gambled after using coke (he's trying to get a double whammy high). The gambling is just as bad as it was before I saw you but coke is too painful to go back to.' (The advance is the coke use has stopped – but natural good feelings are still missing or at least insufficiently abundant: I must revivify them – they're in him but latent, untapped; so far!)

4. *Q: How much pain is it causing you now?* (I focus/directionalise his mind on 'pain' in the present.) A: A lot. I am losing so much

money – I'm losing worse than ever (notice the bookie has no morality about taking his money!) I think I have lost over 10 Grand!' (For US readers a 'grand' is a colloquialism amongst the English working class for £1000/$1558.)

5. *Q: What triggers the gambling?* A: 'The *thrill** that maybe I might hit it big (the key word is THRILL – it's his FEELINGS and imagination; his Gnostic fantasy that illusions could become real. This man is a very vivid visualiser – like all 'junkies'.) I go from low job to a great job now but I keep losing my money. I make more money now but I gamble it away! I don't want to struggle!'

6. *Q: How is your self-worth today?* A: 'Still a problem – I'm not good enough; that's how I feel.' (Now I realise that this is the core of the problem matrix – sh*t! I should have dealt with this last time; oh well, no one's perfect. From speaking to a few of this client's relatives I realise he is being treated like the proverbial 'black sheep of the family'. This is probably a pattern going back into early childhood. Note to parents – over criticise your kids, demand perfection, don't love them unconditionally, attack their self-worth and guess what – YOU may well create a junkie. Well fucking

done. I detect something else from his deflated tone and body language.)

7. *Q: Do you lack self-belief?* A: 'Yes. I can't look at myself in a mirror! (Poor bastard – I will get him to do just that in hypnosis.) I want my self-belief back.' (Good, he had some once – we can use that; everyone has *some* self-belief or they couldn't do so much as brush their teeth! He needs it available in more than just mundane areas of life.)

8. *Q: If you knew that you could only succeed, what would you do with your life?* (I have dragged up lots of painful sh*t. Now is the time to focus him on accessing constructive patterns in his future that HE must create. The first step is to set specific goals and visualise them.) A: 'I want to own my own place. I want to get a terrier (dog). I want normality!' (Bingo! He just gave me his trance word for health – 'normality'. I will use this in the hypnosis part.)

9. *Q: Do you feel you are achieving worthy goals?* (Implying this is important – they move a life forward.) A: 'I need to take action!' (At this point he also tells me about a girl he finds attractive but isn't doing so well with: good sign, he's refocusing on getting genuine pleasure

sources! Yippee! We will work on this in the hypno-part.)

10. *Q: Do you generally feel good? Do you feel more or less miserable than last time?* A: 'Yes I do feel a lot better. No, I am not as unhappy as back then.'

Short and sweet – let's get to it!

Stop taking stupid risks gambling script.

(Deep hypnosis assumed)

Part 1: Layering in good feelings about yourself – acceptance and belief.

Step 1: Re-associating to self-acceptance via permissive hypnosis.

'It's time to ***start to see yourself as you really are...***No one is perfect – we are perfectly imperfect...we have all made mistakes...that's how we ***learn life's lessons...***We all have our native strengths and limitations...that's what being human is all about...we are all different...When you ***view things objectively...***you'll find you are able to ***remain calm as you evaluate yourself fairly...***As an unconditionally loving parent would a child...everyone is a bit naughty from time to time...but you can also allow time to...

focus on your strong points too...we all have them. In this life you have to ***be 100% the real you...***You do some things really well and others not so...So you're just like the rest of us. ***You're ok.*** With the very real knowledge that you can never please everyone...nor is it even desirable to try...you can start to ***feel good about yourself again...***To err is human. No one is SO perfect that they can tell you otherwise...only feel guilty for things you should and then move on...All ***suffering passes...***We ***leave old perceptions behind*** so that to TRY to continue...along a certain path is impossible... At some point we have to ***move on and forgive*** ourselves...As you ***enjoy the process of liking who you are...***and who you were really meant to be...don't be too surprised if you just ***lighten up about so many things...***A good sense of humour helps...

That reminds me of a story...The great hypnotherapist Milton Erickson told a tale about a girl who had been driving in a car...She was so happy and laughing that she tipped her head back...and opened her mouth...At just that moment a seagull flew overhead and accidentally pooped in her mouth! The girl was so embarrassed and ashamed...even though it wasn't her fault...she grew angry, sad, depressed, refused to see friends...So her mother wrote to Erickson and told him the tale of the bird poop incident...Erickson knew just what to do...he didn't hypnotise her...he just wrote a letter saying...'Young girls shouldn't open their mouth so wide when they laugh otherwise birds may well take a poop in them!' And the girl read the letter and was so cross... She told her mother off for not keeping so dreadful a secret...and then the girl just burst out laughing! And she laughed so much she couldn't stop! That's what happens when... ***you see the funny side of things.***

When we admit our limitations...the things we don't excel at...***you are demonstrating confidence, now...***You can in fact ***relax about any and all aspects of who you are...***because that is so attractive a quality.

There is, in a funny way, a perfection in uniqueness...the uniqueness of a moment...the way the trees change colours in autumn...of bright winter light...of warm summer daydreams...of a friend's giggle...the way the sea sounds by the shore, even on passing rainy days...Some people focus on one blemish that they magnify out of all proportion...some ***see the bigger picture...***the woods from the trees...As the saying goes, 'One swallow does not a summer make.' And the simple things like that can ***comfort*** you ***deep inside.***

And if you were able to float into space and look down at the earth...those old ***problems*** would ***diminish in size...*** *(Hypnotic coding: see book 2, Mastering hypnotic language'.)* As you got things in the proper perspective, now...It's important to ***have compassion for yourself*** and deserving others...What if you could learn to believe that...***you are fine just as you are...*** (?) And in turn that led to ***your strengthened self-belief...***What if you... ***Accept your body...Accept your voice... Accept your special mannerisms...Accept your genuine ideas about things...***as being wholly worthwhile and yours...***Accept your strengths and weaknesses...Accept the totality of who you really are*** and hope and wish to be, now...at such a deep and fundamental level of understanding of so many things, anew...

Does a table not accept its table-ness? A dog its dog-ness? The baby its cuteness...the smile its welcoming quality...the fire its warmth...the snow its snow-ball making qualities...Things are what they are...And truth can ***have comfort*** in it...

Beyond your name is the core of who you are... that special place – the marrow of your being... the lifeblood of your expression...the pith of the apple...the fibre of your soul...the clarity of ***your mind in peace...now...***Looking in a mirror and ***seeing the true you reflected back generously...***without prejudice...with deserved approval...with graciousness and amiability...as you would a friend...That's right.

You are a good person...a person of real worth...Many love and care about you...You have touched other's lives positively in ways you can never know...Everyone has a different opinion because they are different...No one is defined by other's opinions of them...Dogs chase their tail because they know no better; you have better things to do. Feel deeply accepting and confident about who you are, noooo-oooow!!!

Per-fect! Let a colour of that feeling wrap itself around you...like warm loving arms - spreading all through you...washing away distortions, deceptions and illusions of the past...Gone for good.

When you ***raise your expectations of what you are truly capable of...***you'll surprise yourself...With this self-acceptance ***you have deep faith in yourself...***which is all confidence really is...As you would encourage a friend in his/her endeavours...as you would lend support to a loved one when needed...You can ***re-start doing that for yourself, now...***You have all the powerful resources within you that you need...to survive, thrive and succeed! Your ***new positive expectations change your life...***and already ***you display self-belief*** in many movements... ***You possess self-belief*** when you do day to day things that we all do... ***You own self-belief*** in all you ever did well... The fact is your were born with self-belief; re-connect to it now! That's great!

These hopes you have for the future are possible when...***you expect more of yourself...***You cannot change the shape of a shoe by expecting it to change...but you can change your outcomes by expecting that more is possible for you...and like a self-fulfilling prophecy ***better things happen...***Our perception of what is possible for us, by us, can and does change as we ***mature...***And it all begins with changing ideas that lead to ***you're talking action to achieve deeply desired goals*** and finding it all so much more easy than you imagined once, back then...All the great achievements of history started as ideas, the ideas became plans, the plans became reality...

You have the power to decide what kind of life you want...Your innovative/creative self or part will help you generate just the right solutions without any conscious effort...Trust yourself...with kindness within too. There is a time and a place to ***take sensible risks*** that move us forward...they keep us feeling alive! But gambling away your needs and future is a pattern that can change now...Whatever the value, the intent of any behaviour...you can

find better ways to realistically satisfy needs...And just knowing that is so liberating... There is a power in ***being free to choose.*** Good feelings – all the good feelings you could ever need exist within you...And your unconscious mind, now, will make more of them thrillingly more available to you so that...you ***start to feel normal again...***That's it.

Because when you decide to ***focus on your goals...***you need to ***remain determined to succeed...***in spite of temporary setbacks... Setbacks are opportunities to find new ways to move forward...***Stay calm, be creative,*** succeed. You need to ***develop an attitude of experimentation*** - you need to ***discover for yourself what you are truly capable of...*** And the good things is, when ***you have full self-acceptance...***inevitably ***your self-belief is rock-solid strong, now...***That's it.

You need only bring your desire to ***be so supportive of your own efforts*** and kindly so...As you pursue any goal you must ***commit to it.*** You must give it your all...you must focus on the here and now...And whatever else needs to be done...will be, by your subconscious mind – trust it to support you powerfully in all your endeavours.

Step 2: Past reframing.

(NFH: By changing how you view the past – you change future perceptions. The perception of the past is mutable as George Orwell knew well.)

Recall a time when you could have used this new self-acceptance. And see yourself in that time – watching it like a movie...That's great... Look at that younger you...Notice everything about them and that place in a detached, calm way...And when you are ready step into that past time and as a wise advisor from the future say something supportive, tell them it all turns out alright...that ***you're completely fine just as you are, now...***Do anything you need to do to...***re-install that deep self-acceptance within you, now.*** I'll be quiet for a full 30 seconds as you do so to your satisfaction... *(Pause etc. In book 9, I will give an extended version of this you can use – this is an old NLP pattern.)*

And that younger you starts to look different... ***feel different...***act different...And **be happy with who you are...**And all these changes ripple through to now...and remain with you... forever: only growing stronger; as new, better pathways of ***self-acceptance and full self-belief return...***in any and all situations...Good feelings have an excuse to grow in such a place...

Step 3: Future pace – dissociated.

With that in mind...imagine a time where you obviously ***hold a more positive outlook...*** knowing you/he *(etc.)* can ***handle any challenge...***learn from it...notice what that you looks like from a distance...how they ***act calmly***...how they are ***focused and determined to succeed...now...***motivated to do well, for THEIR own reasons...and you know what those are...I don't. This is your life to live on your own terms! Maybe you are trying something new...learning something different about yourself that does indeed surprise and delight you...What else can you really do...? The adventure can restart again...All adventures have parts where the hero passes through and beyond tough times and only ***emerges stronger*** from that experience...*(Be quiet for 15 seconds...)*

Step 4: Future pace – associated.

When you are happy with that future you in review...float into that time – it could be 6 months ahead, one or two years...it doesn't matter...Go through that experience and learn from yourself at the deepest levels...See through those eyes of acceptance and belief! Hear through those ears! ***Feel that self-belief***

and acceptance flow all the way through your mind, body, life, now! Amplify that good set of feelings and double it again somehow! That's great! I'll be quiet for a full minute while you ***rehearse success...***in this ***healing*** place...feeling the flow of ***good feelings within...****(Do as you promised.)*

And importantly know, really know that when you ***change deep inside*** others relate to you differently and you like the difference, don't you? Bathe in your new feelings, knowing this is so. Good. Now let's take care of that old pattern of 'gambling'.

Part 2: Gambling dissociation and getting needs satisfied.

Step 5: Directly indirect suggestions to stop gambling.

I'd like to thank your subconscious mind for everything it's done for you...for getting you here safe...for protecting you in all those innumerable ways it does and always will, just better...You did that old gambling habit really well. But you fully realise that although the intent behind it was positive...the results were not so good. You can ***feel the thrill of being alive*** without any external aids...You can ***find better ways to make more money...*** You can ***take sensibly enjoyable risks...***

There are better solutions that lead to satisfaction and you know this. I know you do. So now it's time ***be totally free of that old addictive process...***of any kind, ***now...***it starts with – ***you're being so much more relaxed in general...***As you reconnect to your capacity to take it easy...to ***relax physically and mentally...all the way down...***To therefore ***have more energy*** to devote to the things which deserve it...To ***feel a sublime calm*** that you never thought you had, wasn't it? So things can start working properly...

Step 6: Imagining getting needs met module.

Phase 1: Dissociated rehearsal.

Now you were telling me that you'd like to have a girlfriend. That's great – in an intimate relationship so many of our universal needs get met...not least you ***give quality attention*** and you can ***get quality attention...***With that in mind...just focus on the need to meet the opposite sex...conjure up some scene in your mind – watching it from the outside...a time from your future...when ***this need is being met in a genuinely pleasant and satisfying way...***because you are ***taking action in reality*** to make it so. Your creative part will help you solve any problems that arise...Just get the sense of that time...like having a pleasant daydream...Notice - what you're doing...how that you is feeling...Notice the different responses you are getting...***Relax as you learn from that...***I'll be quiet for 15 seconds or so while you practise that. *(Do so.)*

Good! Now using the ***powerful inner focus*** of this state...Knowing that this relaxation allows your intimate access to ***new creative ideas and associations*** which manifest in delightful and surprising ways...better ones that move you forward...

Phase 2: Associated rehearsal.

When ***you are ready...***Float into that scene... with you getting that need for positive attention from attractive women met...See through those eyes...Hears through those ears...Feel how much ***more confident and light-hearted*** you feel while ***flirting pleasantly...***That better future-present, now...Again I'll be quiet for a full 20 seconds while you go through that...to each and both of your satisfaction.*(Do so.)*

You are learning at deep levels...experientially is the best way. That's right. Good.

Step 7: Parasite reframing and symbology.

(This is really about retraining the general reality orientation to see things as they are! See book 7, 'Escaping cultural hypnosis'.)

Now as you are already feeling better about yourself...let's take a fresh, objective look at the reality of gambling...because gambling is a parasitical thief when you ***view things calmly and objectively...***It stole your time...it stole your self-respect...All that hard-earned cash went to the bookies...You may just as well have flushed it down the toilet or set it on fire... Gambling is a con man – he whispers fanciful promises of wins that will never happen and yet he made it all seem so plausible because ***gambling is a confidence trickster.***

I want you to symbolise that gambling as a person of some kind...The type of person you'd never give the time of day too...the kind of person you would never trust...See that parasite thief over there...reflect now on all that that creature has stolen from you...I'll be silent for 20 seconds as you ***fully ponder that reality...*** *(Do so.)*

Isn't it time to say enough is enough! Isn't it time to ***stop being taken for a ride*** (!?) That was an abusive relationship you had BUT you can ***see through the lies, now.*** In the calmness of this new place, so that... ***new perceptions and responses start to form...***Things, certain things start to re-associate...old associations and ***impulses diminish before they disappear completely, now...***in the light of these tangible realities and realisations about the need to ***FUNDEMENTALLY CHANGE!***

In the past you had focused on the never-never fantasy of gambling's lies...gullibly believed the deceptions...and lies can never be fulfilled...All healthy activities and people enrich your life... Some things and people are givers...others only take. And you ***know which is which, instinctively, now.*** You had focused on 'thrilling feelings' based on hot air...gambling had painted imaginary scenarios in your mind... that never came to be – That gambling creature had hypnotised you and impoverished your life...Imagine that creature whispering to that you over there and know, really know, that ***you never want to experience that gullibility again.***

Step 8: Changing the focus of feelings/associations part 1.

With that in mind...we need for you to ***change certain feelings...***the focus of certain feelings...That fake feeling of the fanciful expectation that occurred *(past tense!)* just before you did what you don't do now needs to be overridden by the reality of that horrible, unpleasant feeling you get *after* you realise that you have been made a fool of...Maybe you can recall a time you were on the way to lay a bet... And you have that fanciful thrill that once led you to throw good money after bad...And as that feeling starts...***refocus your mind now!*** Get a vivid sense of that rotten, lousy feeling you get after you realise you just blew your hard earned cash...

My God it feels rough to be there, doesn't it? You can't believe what you did. What you used to do. Almost as if...***that's not the real you.*** Get in touch with that post gambling feeling that you hate so much...Really ***experience the reality of the consequences*** of that...What could you have done with that money? *(A beat only after each question...)* What experiences did you miss out on? Where could you have gone? Who might you have met? What better things could you have done with your precious time and cash? Wasted! So it's time to ***really alter those old responses, now... unconsciously...***And I'll show you how!

(This is an advanced N.A.C pattern – you evoke the behaviour and use rapid time-distortion to re-associate unpleasant feelings to the action; geddit! This can be used for many addictions. See the final analysis part below.)

Step 9: Changing the focus of feelings/associations part 2 – directly indirect suggestions.

Once again, I am speaking to you, the subconscious mind – I would like to thank you for everything you've done to help and look after this person...You made this person gamble...You had reasons...You were *trying* to help them satisfy needs...but you know now that ***there are better ways to get your needs met...***You know it's best to ***stop that gambling trance from ever occurring, now...***that's what's best for this person in their life right now, is it not? Whenever this person even so much as thinks about gambling as they once did...whenever they encounter an old trigger...you can ***instantly feel that horrible feeling in place of the old excited one.***

You can consider the consequences of any action realistically...You can ***get that unpleasant consequences feeling even before anything else takes place...***This will happen automatically if this person even thinks about gambling again...That's their 100% total personal reality...They can still ***take calculated risks*** that move life forward, that's fine but... the old feeling was a lie...the old feeling was an illusion...it's time to ***create new choices...***it's time to do healthier things to get needs met... and your creative part will help you...In fact the very idea of gambling seems ludicrous, ridiculous...like something that wouldn't, couldn't happen in this person's life... the very idea of it is unreal – and it won't happen. ***Old feelings are replaced by new ones, now!*** Old, unhelpful trances fade away and only a wakeful, knowing awareness remains. Old triggers and associations have no power whatsoever. ***No obsessions, no impulses*** to anything other than healthier choices...***No problem whatsoever!***

Step 10: Wire-in new associations fully.

In a moment I will say 'Twilight!' When I do, that will be your signal to do the following... One after another – associated into those times, imagine 3 separate examples of times in the past when you felt the urge to gamble...

- As soon as that old thrilling feeling/excitement starts it is swamped and smothered by the horrible feelings. They just come over you just like that (snap fingers!)
- You really ponder all the things you'll lose out on.
- And then you imagine what you'll do differently to get genuine needs met. Okay you ready? I'll be quiet for a full minute and a half which is plenty of

time in trance for you to ***reset old responses with the new, now...***

- I'll repeat that: 1. See an old situation through your own perspective. 2. Old actions are swamped by bad feelings. 3. Ponder negative consequences. 4. Imagine better solutions. Again: 1. See that time as a participant in it. 2. Old actions are swamped by bad feelings. 3. Ponder negative consequences. 4. Imagine better solutions. Okay – ready?

'Twilight!!!' Go through those times and new responses now, in the pause...*(Quiet for a full minute and a half!)*

Good. Re-associations are occurring – Reconfigurations...Rewiring...Reconnections... New responses...And anything else you know that needs to be adjusted to help this person fulfil their needs as a total person...***Re-organisations of already existing subconscious structures happen right now...***in the best, safe and healthiest ways possible! You ***feel normal, now!*** You have knowing feelings that ***a profound change has occurred.*** You can take this hypnotic act as sign and a genuine signal that this is so.
You are a happy healthy person now – you are ***fully in control*** and you realise with appropriate pride and clarity that it was one of

the best decisions you ever made – ***your life is enriched*** in all senses of that word from now on. Good.

Step 11: Future pace the new you.

Now just imagine a time in your much better future that fully confirms ***this has worked...*** Might be with friends or family? Who knows? You do! See yourself in a dissociated way, as an observer...watching that relaxed, happy you... doing some things that are much better and rewarding for you... ***You are free!*** See how that you is definitely getting needs and wants met properly in ways that ONLY enhance your life and move it forward...*(Pause 15 secs.)*

Well done! Now, when you are happy with the new set of responses...float into the free and independent you! See through those insightful eyes! Feel the ***freedom and clarity in mind and body!*** Hear through the ears of freedom and control! You only hear sensible messages... You don't thumb suck anymore you outgrew it! ***Feel those wonderful feelings spread*** throughout mind and body now! Lock them in, ***lock these magnificent changes in, now*** and keep them as a gift to yourself. Excellent! You are doing great – we are almost done!

Step 12: Reflecting things as they are module.

(You linguistically fractionate the person from observer to participant by the use of pronouns 'That person' and 'You'.)

Dissociated – see yourself looking at a reflection of you in some surface that shows you as you are...That's it, and know...That person deserves a good life...That person can give and receive positive attention...That person has many wonderful qualities...That person has more to discover...That person can and does ***feel good naturally!*** That person esteems themselves and expects to be treated with respect...That person can make better choices...That person is so confident and calm to the core! Their powerful subconscious mind aids them in all their efforts. Trust it!

Associated – see a reflection of you in some surface that shows you as you are...That's it, and know...you deserve a good life...You can give and receive positive attention...You have many wonderful qualities...You have more to discover...You can and do ***feel good naturally!*** You esteem yourself and expect to be treated with respect...You can ***make better choices...*** You are ***so confident and calm to the core!*** You ***feel so happy!*** Your powerful subconscious mind aids you in all your efforts. Trust it! Well done! And now I'll begin the waking up process etc....'

(Begin wake up protocol of choice etc.)

<u>*Analysis of process.*</u>

- Build self-belief and acceptance.
- Get client to visualise healthy alternatives to get genuine need satisfaction.
- Parasite symbology dissociation. Ham up the negative symbolism – this is N.A.C* (Neuro-Associative-Conditioning) – see below.
- Revivify and amp up negative associations and <u>*post hypnotically*</u> link them to triggers inside and out. You can use this protocol for porn etc. too. As I said, this is really a quite sophisticated example of N.A.C as outlined in several of my other books. You take the existing 'strategy' which was: **trigger - excitement - act - regret - loop** and turn it into **trigger - regret - new act - feel good - exit.** Very simple structure when you break it all down.
- Wrap up process: 'see self realistically visualisation' and ego-boost

suggestions.

One of the rewards of effective therapy is – the elated high you get when it all goes fine and dandy! You have helped your fellow man or woman: somehow the world is a fraction bit better; the positive consequences of helping this person are all the many beneficial ripple effects that will spread through his or her social networks from now on. You did a good deed. Give yourself a pat on the back.

(*N.A.C or 'Neuro-Associative-Conditioning' is fully explained in my 3rd book 'Powerful hypnosis' – in essence it is about changing a person's habitual sets of associations for new ones. In hypnotic trance this process is quicker and more vigorous.)

The two hijacked parts of addiction.

The defiant/rebel/mutinous part is hijacked by drugs and the steadfast/stubborn/rule-keeper part is its accomplice in stupidity. Both keep you on a given path that you think is yours and maintain addictive processes. They maintain the drug tyranny when they are supposed to do the exact opposite! Although many forms of hypnotic interventions as detailed in this book can powerfully help addicts - none work so powerfully as interventions that 'talk' to and negotiate with these two parts. Again: get them on board in change work and victory is assured. They will help re-directionalise the brain toward health. I have seen it happen again and again. Think about that though: addictive processes/drugs steal your mind's capacity for independent volition like an evil hypnotic parasite. And people think drugs are 'cool'.

Is A.A a cult?

I have had several clients who were involved with Alcoholics Anonymous (A.A) and its equally weird offshoots like Cocaine Anonymous (C.A.) etc. The so-called '12 Step Plan' of A.A. is to my mind very similar to, though less intense, a cult-like indoctrination process. It has nothing to do with reality or getting free of any addictive habit disorder. I have written about the myths regarding addictions promoted by various 'Rehab Centres' etc. in my other books – again I see cult-like processes at work. I will quickly run over the A.A/C.A myths now and debunk them...

- *'You are a drunk/junkie for life etc.!'* No you are not; you have merely started using something to experiment/cope and for various reasons your subconscious is looping the habit; it's a protective mechanism to help you deal with stress, worry, trauma, life etc. With skilled hypnosis you will be free for life. The 'therapy cults' want *permanent* growing membership – any honestly motivated help group would want you independent ASAP!
- *'You have to reach rock bottom to change!'* Bullshit! You just have to want to change now and hypnosis will

work; if the hypnotherapist knows what he or she is doing.

- *'My name is x and I am a y!'* This act is part of the process of conning you that addiction is part of your genetic identity. No scientific evidence this is so. I have 'cured' far too many 'addicts' I'm afraid. This is known as an 'overt act' – used by cults in the programming process. See, 'Forbidden hypnotic secrets', 'Wizards of trance' and 'Escaping cultural hypnosis' for the low down on cults.

- *You hang around with people who have drug problems like you.* You should hang around healthy people!

- *The belief that you take it 24 hours at a time* presupposes *failure!*

- *The 12 steps* are hypnotic because it is *suggested* you follow them.

- *Believing in a 'higher power'* is no good for atheists. In fact an atheist successfully sued A.A for violating his beliefs! Unless you are a mental contortionist: one man convinced himself his radiator was a higher power. Ok-ay!

- *Handing over 'salvation' to a higher*

power presupposes that YOU aren't responsible for changing! Never heard the phrase – 'God helps those who help themselves,'?

- *Interesting note:* like the cult explosions of the 1970's Catholics make up a majority of A.A members. The rape and destruction of Catholicism proper in the 20th century was a major cause (see book 7).

The 'A.A cult-lite' keeps you dependent on it – talking to 'someone' or some group about using drugs does nothing. You need to replace the old associations and patterns in the brain and loop healthy responses to life, unconsciously. Only hypnosis can do that in 1 session folks. Admittedly A.A is not the most dangerous cult-like organisation in the world (political parties are cult-lite after all!) but it still functions quite a bit like one.

Addiction 'counselling' is barmy (crazy!).

When someone seeks help for addictions they want to get off the drug etc. - that day! You don't dig up trauma from the past – that makes people feel worse (see 'Powerful hypnosis' for thorough specifics on this). You don't need to talk about problems any longer than it takes to craft the hypnotic solutions. The addiction quiz in this book is sufficient. You wanna help people or not? If a client is suffering from anxiety, depression and/or trauma you treat it with hypnotherapy – see book 9 for full details.

What is a 'relapse'?

So-called 'relapses' are caused by a few things:

- A life stressor/loss.
- Not getting your universal human needs met.
- Not being ready to commit to change.
- Continuing with an unhealthy lifestyle in general.
- Hanging out with a loser druggie crowd (your 'associates' – geddit?).

That's it. The first 3 being the most common.

Case 4: Booze 1 - a bog-standard drink moderation session.

When I first started in hypnotherapy most of my addiction clients were smokers; after the then UK Government of David Cameron's Conservatives started harping on about the need for Britain to ditch its 'booze culture', the effectiveness of such propaganda soon worked its magic and my practice was full of middle aged women wanting to cut down on drinking. Most were 1 bottle of wine a night ladies which was admittedly too much. Cause? Stress! Mainly of 'juggling' home and job were usually to blame – drink was a wind-down and a lone treat after a hectic day's onslaught of duties. Most of these women were simply overworked and exhausted. Career *and* children come at a price. With some there were underlying self-esteem issues to solve. But sorting out a drink moderation session is easy! Below I show you 2 alternative ways of doing it. ***Note for puritanical therapists etc.: moderate drinking should be the goal of all drink related sessions unless the client 100% wants to stop altogether. Teetotalism is not required or necessary. There is evidence moderate alcohol consumption protects the brain from Alzheimer's.***

Alternative 1: Basic drink moderation script – directly indirect/authoritarian example.

(For years I worked only with authoritarian hypnosis with great success – especially with drink moderation: an example of a 2nd session 'top up' follows...As always deep hypnosis assumed)

'Now once again, I'm speaking to you...the subconscious mind...You are fully in control. I'd like to thank you for all progress achieved; for all the positive changes that you have made in this lady's life. Even just ***drinking a bit less*** is improvement. *(In authoritarian hypnosis you do not have to use embeds. However I find they improve all styles of hypnotic work massively!)* For showing her more of what she is really capable of, to whatever degree. For everything you have done to protect and look after her, for having moderated her alcohol consumption in that helpful way you have. For having helped her ***make those changes*** and more but again she wants to ***progress even more,*** she has set a direction that she wishes to continue along, not temporarily or in fits and starts but smoothly, easily and ***making improvements permanently,*** to a greater degree, ***now.***

So much better choices, behaviour changed in just the right way for her own unconscious reasons, actually living life more healthily in the way this lady wants. You are the part that had been generating the old habit, the past urge for excessive alcohol of any kind up until now. And yes, you have had your many reasons, for maintaining those former habits, that's all they were, the old habitual pattern of behaviour, that past conditioning – that old way of coping of a younger self doing their best with the choices that they used to perceive they had. Wouldn't it be better, much better to ***keep the positive intent of that behaviour but find new ways, healthier ways to satisfy that, now?***

As you are obviously very good at automatically running certain habits for this lady, isn't it finally time to make lasting changes, to ***drink less and less alcohol.*** Sooner or later we all change, do we not? Solidify those changes, add to them, with better feelings. *(Building in good feelings is vital for success with addictions.)* You produce all her good moods, her wonderful feelings. Her sense of ***mental and physical relaxation, now...***Because you are the seat of her emotions and you can ***make her feel, really feel better*** in daily life. Altering things at just the right rate and speed, certain perceptions, attitudes, choices changing, ***increase her inner strength*** *(negotiate with 'inner strength' and boost it too! Note: with this lady I did not use any complex negotiation* *procedure; direct hypnosis alone can work...)* and dominance and power over those old outmoded ways of doing things. I know and you really know that ***you do have that ability.***

We now know it's time to, ***make a decision and stick to it,*** to ***stop drinking so much alcohol,*** of any kind – to, ***become a moderate drinker, now.*** That's right! It's her new identity, it's what she needs; what this person/lady/man truly, deeply wants for themselves/herself etc. in her life at this time and in her ***much more relaxed and positive future.*** She has made a conscious decision and she wants your help unconsciously to achieve this now; it's who she wants to be, it's how she proceeds to develop and you know that the old misuse of alcohol of any kind is no longer what is in her best and highest interests. It's not something that can ***add a needed sense of security,*** not a satisfying or great choice, not invigorating at all for this woman. Doesn't make them bright-eyed and bushy-tailed! She wants to ***be habitually sober,*** without those hangovers, without the fears, anxiety, worry – gone; she is totally fed up of not feeling her/his best. She wants to ***feel at her best*** at any given moment. You recognise now - that is no longer what's right for this lady; you realise that is not what she needs to be healthful and fresh, to ***have mental clarity...*** Not in any area of her life.

It had upset her emotionally. She could ***feel better physically.*** It had troubled her mentally. It had adversely affected her relationships with others. And who were you not really anyway that is ***a much calmer, relaxed, moderate drinker?*** Anyway a better way but back then, any wise response but that one then and ***only these new choices...***

Know, really know, deeply, that what is *honestly* better for her is to ***really reduce her/his alcohol consumption now,*** permanently. Setting that better path – that powerful new direction, *she* has chosen. *(Tonally underline that it's 'their' choice and not your imposition.)* ***Excessive alcohol consumption becomes a part of the past, now.*** Better, healthier ways can fulfil that intent. Not someone who even thinks or obsesses about buying wine/beer or anything else for that matter. Purchases more healthy food and drink products at the shops/stores. ***She/he is a moderate drinker, now.*** And because ***she/he is a moderate drinker,*** there are absolutely ***no urges, no desires, no cravings*** for any/too much alcohol at all, ever.

This strong-minded, determined lady is ***sensibly moderating their drinking...***That's it! Doesn't want alcohol to be a dominant part of her life anymore. It was like a relationship that just wasn't going anywhere good, now. So there will be no past patterns of excessive wine/beer/booze etc. or whatever she drank in the past on any occasion, ***purchasing habits can and do change,*** we can ***easily change habits*** when fully motivated to do so. And I know ***her total motivation to change is very strong*** is it not? So ***no excess booze*** of any kind and so no hangovers too; just much ***more abundant relaxation and confidence. Now,*** isn't it nice to know you can ***relax without alcohol*** (?) You can ***feel good naturally...***Better feelings more and more and more at those times that she needs to ***feel that better way...***

And you know - profoundly - that there will not even be any patterns of thinking as there were in the past, with regards to these changing habits and this is so. Those old responses just don't apply to a woman who is ***in control;*** who can honestly say ***you're in control, now.*** Those things don't harmonise with the reality of ***being a moderate drinker, now...***and that's who she wants to be from now on.

And if this person is around friends, relatives, colleagues, or in environments, situations or places that would have triggered the old response, it can trigger healthier ones instead, now. If anyone else is drinking too much alcohol and even if she's had a tiring, perhaps mildly stressful day it won't and can't concern her in any way at all, she is more than capable of ***unconsciously rediscovering what satisfies that intent healthily;*** her creative part will help, will it not? Will it not? She can, you will ***relax after work – naturally…***She'll ***feel calm.*** She thinks and feels and lives as moderate drinkers do, chooses that which reflects a moderate drinker's lifestyle, has ***no urge*** to return to the less than 100% healthy actions of the past.

It's time to ***make a firm resolution,*** really make it and then ***stick to it.*** I know that you know how to ***make the right decisions.*** Knowing there actually are consequences to our actions. They just don't affect us either; knowing that the fake expectation that alcohol can *really* satisfy any part of you was and is a false one: an illusion. Like a dream fading away…now…And so a part of this lady can remind her of all the good reasons that she did change, haven't you? It's finally ***time for a change,*** so she can ***feel healthy and sober, now.*** And ***keep these changes too*** and not with a sense of deprivation but with ***a wonderful feeling of health, clear-headedness,*** the genuine satisfaction of her healthy needs more and more and more.

In fact the very idea, conception of mis-using or

abusing alcohol in the past just seems wholly laughable, incongruous and off the wall, out of character and comically unbelievable! Something that doesn't occur in her new reality – It's beyond the scope of anything really routine, habitual and natural, it really is. Because when we ***deeply want to change*** the power of the unconscious mind can assist us when it's right.

The smell of any alcohol, the sight of a glass or bottle of wine/beer or any other form of booze is ***no problem***, irrelevant, indifferent. The sight of wine in a shop – just feeling the urge to pass on and ***buy something else.*** No bother at all. No longer going into a supermarket trance but ***fully aware of what is being bought and the consequences on health of each purchase.***

If anyone offers this lady even a sip or a glass of alcohol, beyond their healthy limits - she can ***STOP!*** It is simply the most natural, easy thing in the world to ***respond calmly and confidently, indifferently or otherwise*** using just the right words and attitude spontaneously...Feeling that same sense of resolve...in the evenings. Perhaps on her own too? *(These were her triggers.)* The ***good feelings are there X.*** *(X = client's name.)* Reconnect to them unconsciously, now. And as ***this just happens automatically...***

every time ***you make progress...***and acknowledge every success however slight, or great. Change can be heroic or gradual. Whatever each and both of you prefer; you will ***indulge and reward this much happier woman with a great feeling of success and accomplishment...***a very good feeling for being a moderate drinker. We can all ***resist the temptation to do certain things*** that weren't right and good for us...because we actually, honestly acknowledged the consequences, didn't you?

Confident, much happier, calmer, determined! A strong-minded women! ***Find this process easy,*** before you know it, without knowing how you did it, it's just a part of your improved patterns, choices, real choices in living how you wish, a part of your new identity, confident in that decision, confident in the actual ability to ***carry it out, now.***

You ***believe in yourself*** permanently, throughout her much healthier life. No matter what the ups and downs from this moment on. *(This person had 'relapsed' after a personal crisis.)* Sometimes we do stumble, wobble, we are human! ***Forgive yourself...***You are perfectly imperfect as we all are. But descended from millennia of survivors and that fact gives you strength; sometimes we do have to take two steps back to ***take that great leap***

forward, and as we land we find ***the stability is there,*** it always was, taking it all in her stride, no matter how things change, and they will, trusting herself...all-ways...now...

If you can cut back a little bit...you can ***cut back a bit more.*** And a bit more after that and a bit more and more and more. Gradual... or sudden...improvements. One day. One week. Month. Year. Decade. Before you know it... ***Feeling so good...***

Lock in changes.

Your unconscious mind will begin to finalise and ***lock in these gains permanently now.*** Any and all adjustments that are needed to this woman's feelings, attitudes, ideas, beliefs and values, cravings, urges, desires – healthier, occur! Lifestyle choices, activity levels, perceptions, ability to ***relax in better ways,*** energy levels boosted! Appropriate focus and concentration, motivation and willpower, determination, discipline and persistence! Levels of responsibility, arousal and comfort levels, ability to ***feel good natural feelings naturally,*** communications, new associations, re-associations, re-organisations of already existing subconscious structures, building upon past suggestions, gains, progress, enhancing them to the point where ***they become a part of a new set of responses,*** identity and individuality, and anything else you really know needs to be fine-tuned and modified in just the right ways and to the precise degree...to allow this woman/person to ***really be a moderate drinker, now, and forever, permanently for the rest of their life*** – a happy and healthy individual, so much more ***confident*** in this certain success! Past positive ways returned and yet enhanced further and grown even stronger, better, a higher level of functioning with a clean bill of health. Finally liberated from any old unhelpful, unhealthy habits...***all right now.*** Making better short, medium and long term decisions in all areas of her life, now. Positivity feeding back on itself over and over again; completing the process right now.

You will make these rectifications, improvements and more, make them habitual... assisting this healthy woman to ***remain a moderate drinker,*** loosing excess weight healthily as a consequence. *(The client was worried about drink related weight gain – beer belly etc.; use that!)* Changing as swiftly as is desirable and feasible, realistically, in the next few seconds. Changing in the most sensible and beneficial ways only...Make it all so effortless. Accept as you totally comprehend at all levels of mentation/processing...that ***these changes have been made.*** *(Pause a beat...)* ***Excellent! You are really doing well!'***

(You can sling in some wrapping up work etc. of your choice and then begin waking the client up! Pretty straight forward – no future pacing or more complex visualisations, dissociations, negotiations etc. you just politely tell the subconscious – ***you did that, now do this!*** *Authoritarian/direct styles are covered in book 4, 'Forbidden hypnotic secrets' and 6, 'Crafting hypnotic spells' in depth.)*

Now a different approach...

Alternative 2: Basic drink moderation script – permissive, NLP-ish and 'Ericksonian' example.

(Deep hypnosis assumed!)

'The fact is your body has a wisdom...it knows when you have had too much of anything...it sends you certain signals that you had been ignoring up until now...And to a certain extent, a little bit of overindulgence now and again is okay...it's good to let go and have fun from time to time...but not every day can be party time can it? So as you relearn to ***notice what your body is telling you...***as you relearn to ***relearn a habit of moderation and control, now...***

As we mature some things become more important than others, do they not? Our tastes change...the kind of people we want to associate with alters...we may devote more or less attention to this and not that, now...The secret in - ***you're becoming a moderate drinker, now...***is that there is no secret to ***relearn self-control...***there is no secret to ***stopping at a certain sensible limit...***there is no secret that when you ***have several drink free nights*** a week...so you ***feel much better in yourself...***Waking in the morning with that clear, drink-free mind and more...feeling so healthy and productive...

There is a time in life when you can just have too much of anything...we've all had times like that...too much sugar makes something sickly sweet...too much food leaves you bloated... doing the same things over and over can be boring...We all have had times when we just thought...***enough is enough...***have we not?

It's nice to enjoy a drink...maybe you like a glass of wine to ***wind down...*** (?) Maybe it's a pint of beer with friends... (?) it can help you ***relax and socialise*** and that's fine...We need to consider the consequences of our actions if we indulge in that which we shouldn't too often...I have a friend who says life is so short... I say life is LONG and consequences matter...We all need to make better short, medium and long term decisions...we have a sense of responsibility to ourselves and others, do we not? People say, 'Live in the now!'

I say enjoy this moment and know that you need to take care of the future too...

Negative consequences associations zip!

(By playing around with time in trance you can create unconscious processing re-associations.)

What if you were merely thinking of having even one too many and ZIIII-IIIP! You know what it's like to wake up feeling sluggish and just not right after a few too many...recall a time like that...Urgh! It doesn't feel nice at all does it? You think – 'What did I do that for!?' Do you want to feel like that more often? About the same? Or ***do it less often, now...***

You wouldn't order a favourite meal and smother it with your favourite sauce! You wouldn't put too much cream in a cake! You wouldn't listen to the same speech over and over and over...You don't walk around and around in circles...at some point...you ***tire of certain things.*** You want a break. You need a ***change...***When ***you take days off the booze...***paradoxically you enjoy it more and you don't get such bad hangovers...Sometimes when you regularly moderate your drinking... you don't really get much of a hangover at all... But a hangover is a signal that says – ***enough is enough!*** And the night before, you reached a point when you should have stopped...from now on stopping is easy...and you have many private conscious and unconscious reasons why this must be so...

There is a time when we all need to act more sensibly...doesn't mean we stop having fun...in fact you'll ***have more fun as a result!*** You do not want a toxic build-up of booze in your system...you want to ***listen to your body's wisdom...***

Positive future pace – dissociated objective viewing.

See yourself in a time and a place when ***you control your drinking...***You're doing whatever you do...but notice ***at a key point you stop...****(Pause for 10 secs or so.)*

Choose another time to view...Maybe you are alone having a relaxing few...you're doing whatever it is you do...but recognise that ***at a key point you stop...***You know, really know inside that...***that's enough of that...***But say it wilfully in your own words. That's it! *(Pause for 10 secs to allow processing...)*

No one is saying live like a monk just ***live more healthily...***No one is saying never drink, just ***drink a bit less...***In any situation you can ***maintain your right to choose...***You ***have behavioural flexibility...now...***If you were to try in vain to have one more when you know you shouldn't just recall the morning after the night before...***Remember the consequences of certain actions at the key point...****(Allow 10 secs etc.)*

And once you have considered that...Get a feel of what it's like to wake up alcohol free, clear-minded and sober! Ah! ***Feel that lovely difference*** and proceed towards not that but this, now...It's where and what you want in your life at this key point, is it not? *(Pause for 10 secs...)*

Like watching a movie – see a time where you are turning down an extra drink offered...Maybe friends are saying – 'Go on: one more won't hurt!' But you know your own mind. You know your own body. You make your own decisions about your health. Some things must be more prioritised than others, now. See yourself politely decline because ***you have regained control,*** have you not? Will you not? Didn't you? That's it! *(10 secs etc.)*

Great! You don't listen to old voice mail over and over as ***some messages are irrelevant...***the time is passed that. You can ***enjoy days off...***you can ***socialise without alcohol...***

Associated self-imitation.

In a moment not yet but soon, I want you to imagine floating into your body and ***going through a whole day alcohol free!*** Get firmly in touch with that lovely clear-headed morning feeling! Go through the whole day experiencing how good you feel...So much healthier that it feels truly amazing! You can do that as I am quiet for a full minute...and you have all the time you need to ***learn in trance*** that which you need...Go through that when I say – 'Go for it!' And...'Go for it!' *(Be quiet for 1 minute.)*

Associate into a night in control.

Good. Now see yourself over there...Maybe it's a night out? Certainly a time that confirms ***this has worked, now...***And go through that night start to finish...by floating into yourself and ***experiencing control as a moderate drinker!*** That's great! Feel how good that feels to - see through those eyes! Hear through those ears! To ***feel that self-control and total willpower, now!*** Feel this in every fibre of your being even if you have had a drink or two. Take a while to ***enjoy this process*** while I'm quiet! *(Pause for 30 seconds.)*

You see...you know, really know how to do what you need to...at a very deep level of mind.

Good. Now, to help you ***re-associate to your unconscious resources in new contexts...*** let's build in ***total will power at those key moments*** of choice...

(If you read book 7 you'll know that hypnosis shuts down the executive function of the brain: the part that supplies your sense of volition or 'willpower'; this is why addictions are hypnotic by nature! We are snapping the client out of alcohol trance just at the point when his or her will is essential.)

Will power on command anchor/trigger.

1. Access resource and create anchor/trigger.

Some people come to see me and they say stuff like...'I lack willpower.' But they had the willpower to come and see me...so that means ***you have willpower already...***It's just that in the past you hadn't had access to it so readily at certain times and places...But if ***you have willpower*** here...there is no reason why you can't ***have it at necessary times too...***With that in mind...

Please recall a time in your life when you felt indomitable willpower! Great...Be fully back in that time...See what you saw...Hear what you heard...***Feel that total willpower flowing through mind and body!*** Absorb and immerse yourself in that experience. That's right.

Good. Now make that image bigger, brighter, bolder – make it panoramic! Take those sounds and make them fuller and richer, more vivid and stereo! Amp up those feelings of ***your indomitable willpower, now!*** *(A beat)* Double those feelings! *(A beat...)* Double them again!

And at the peak of that feeling of willpower say an associative word in your mind only... and/or squeeze together a thumb and forefinger on a preferred hand! *(Option.)* That's it!

And as you do that...***you have created a deep neurological link...***In order to ***have this feeling at key moments*** of choice all you need to is fire off that trigger... Let's practise that...

2. Future pace resource on command.

Imagine as if you are in that old time feeling a slight urge to drink too much...and before it has time to grow fire off that trigger and ***feel that indomitable willpower smother that completely...***Because, when you are in just the right frame of mind when you need to be... you can do anything positive, realistic and healthy...and this is so.

You may not even have to carry out a trigger... You may find ***these timely feelings are there for you...***These powerful feelings remain with you...You have a knowing feeling that things have changed for the better without knowing the exact mechanics.

Summation suggestions.

Key moments become so much easier and easier...and you feel more and more healthy and in control...No longer a puppet or a slave... You've snapped out of that unhelpful trance at key times...because you are pulling the strings, are you not? No one and nothing can bully you...***you are a moderate drinker...***all you need is within...you use alcohol wisely...the thought of doing anything else is completely outside of your new experience...No longer a part of a moderate drinker's reality.

And that is who you are...What you do...It is part of your identity...You can ***relax and feel confident at key moments...***Such people are very attractive indeed...***feel a very tangible sense of deep reassurance*** knowing this is so. Any and all re-organisations of already existing subconscious structures occurs, now! That's it!'

(Do more change work, wake up etc. Up to you! In this script we have taken an existing strategy of not considering long term-consequences and made the opposite of that happen at all key moments; and not only that we have built in a state of willpower at key moments when previously it was inaccessible. Quite straight forward.)

Additional module: personalised suggestions.

Clients often ask for help with things not obviously related directly to the 'presenting problem'; in reality they are – they are part of the problem matrix. For example a man came to see me for help in stopping smoking. He also wanted me to boost his self-confidence as he had not 'adjusted to going bald!' He and his wife had ambitions to write for film and TV so I boosted his confidence and creativity in that respect too. You can interweave such work as you deal with the main problem/goal. I usually do now and again. And/or you can lob in a module after the main body of change work when you tackle such small side issues. Some example suggestions for the man above follow; this is your chance to do impro! An essential skill for a hypnotist.

'You can know that baldness is a sign of increased testosterone and masculinity. Attractiveness is about how you feel about

yourself. Some women find bald men very attractive.' **<u>A truthful reframe.</u>**

'Everyone is creative. We all know how to write and tell stories – you've been doing it your whole life. Use these creative abilities to write your own stories. Sit down and just write – don't edit. Just create. When you have the first draft finished then you can check it and improve it on the second etc.' **<u>A reframe that he already is a writer he just doesn't know it plus some specific skills for overcoming 'writers block' (actually just a lack of confidence!). This is why to be a successful hypnotist you must have a wide knowledge base beyond just hypnosis!!!</u>**

Case 5: Booze 2 - treating severe 'alcoholism'.

Real 'alcoholism' is about self-obliteration. With all so-called 'alcoholics' there is always underlying trauma and depression in my experience. This must be treated before you have a prayer of touching the addiction. Once the pain of extreme anxiety and the open emotional wounds of past suffering are gone – the addiction will have no present purpose and the subconscious will relinquish it. 'Alcoholics' are sanely self-medicating – if they didn't they may well suffer a full nervous breakdown, experience depression with psychotic phases or worse. Again book 9, 'Hypnotically annihilating anxiety!' will teach you how to clear up the other mess easily; and I do mean easily. Anxiety has a code and I've cracked it!

Alcohol numbs emotional pain, even of the most savage kind. When the alternative is nothing, the subconscious is doing the best it can in dire circumstances, primarily based on doctors and head-shrinkers (of varying hues) total inability to do anything practical and fast. As this book is focusing solely on addiction deprogramming padawans, we will only deal with the addiction beating part in the next script; a script that will help you 'CURE' alcoholism. Unlike all the other books that tease you with promises to teach you x, y and z but do not deliver (I know; I read 'em and tried 'em!), my books are written to get results! I have done this many times – you can too.

NOTE: with both moderate drinking and stopping alcoholism you need to use the 2nd parts negotiation script in this book if you wish to be 100% certain of success – see the cocaine addiction section. It is the most important step; have I mentioned that?!!: the following script just backs it up. Often I have used the parts negotiation alone for mild addictions and that works fine, but my motto is, 'Better too much than not enough.' I bombard the problem away! People have paid me their hard earned money: I owe them to succeed.

Beat 'alcoholism' script.

Step 1: Activating a rebellion!

'I am now speaking to the part that is in charge of this behaviour and process. Up until this moment you had been using alcohol for a set of reasons that were once valid...but now there are better responses...better ways...better ideas...better behaviours and choices...that you can chose to operate from. In order for you to ***do this successfully...***I would like you to recall a time when you felt strong and determined...A time you felt you could ***stand up for yourself*** and did so effectively. That's it.

Perhaps it was a time when you needed to ***rebel...*** A time the rebel part of you felt like it had to stand up to something that wasn't in your interests. *(Pause for 3-5 secs.)*

When you have that time – see through those eyes! Hear through those ears! Feel that sense of power and determination flooding through you! That's right! Make the memory of that time bigger and brighter! Turn up the sounds! Feel those feelings of determination to ***take a stand, now*** flowing through you! That's it!

Turn those feelings into a colour! Let that colour become brighter and more intense and as you do that... ***these powerful feelings only grow within you.*** Lock them in and keep them as a gift for yourself. You have certain knowing feelings that help you do this. Good.

Step 2: The importance of drying out.

You had been harming certain organs: the liver, stomach, brain. In order for all parts of you to work optimally you need give them a break. You need to let them do what they do best. You need to ***care for yourself...*** And when you do you'll find they can repair themselves naturally...they know how...You just need to ***start to treat your whole self with respect...*** As you would a new born baby – with a sense of 100% responsibility.

And in order to ***act in this new way...***You need a part of you to ***calm right down inside...***because when you are calm you simply make better decisions...When ***you are very calm*** – you pay attention to feedback from your mind and body...

Every authoritarian regime collapses in the end...enough people ***become sick of the old ways of being.*** The nature of man is that he doesn't like being bullied. Plants do not like too much water...there is the right amount of anything. *(A repetitive theme of my work is the idea of 'balance'.)* Everything has its limits.

Water is needed for life and that booze/alcohol had been dehydrating you...The fact is that booze promises what it can't deliver...like a cheap door to door salesman. It's not possible to achieve the impossible, is it? Just because someone tells you that you could sprout wings and fly doesn't mean that those words = reality, does it? It is better to ***attend to healthier messages...***

And I know there is a part of you that looks out for manipulation...it looks out for ways others might lie to you or lead you astray...And that part can notice when a pattern is working for you...or against you. Now, there is an old saying...'If you always do what you always did, you'll always get what you always got.' *(By implication you are politely saying: 'CHANGE IDIOT!!!')*

With all these understandings in mind you now know that what is right for this person now is to ***be sober.*** The best thing for this person is to ***moderate their drinking*** to healthy levels...to ***feel in control.*** There is a time when ***you need a break from alcohol*** altogether...A time to ***dry out*** and let that body recover. No matter what triggered that old response...you can ***cope in better ways...***and when you ***remain calm and confident*** about life's challenges...***your creative part starts to generate solutions.***

As your curious unconscious finds a way to make these changes your own you can ***enjoy the prospect of waking up clear headed and sober*** – ah! Can you recall a time like that? When you awoke ***calm and optimistic, feeling good about life.*** That's it – simply do what you've already done, wasn't it? Now. That's right.

As you ***start to feel stronger*** than you've ever felt...you can know, really know...that you start to ***ignore old signals and urges...*****Now,** I know there were times when you once felt that you needed the booze to cope with certain events *(x, y and z etc.).* The intent was positive and we must respect that. I would like to thank what we call ***you're unconscious...***for all it did to look after and protect you BUT...there are far better ways you can choose...It's time to ***decouple old associations...***What once seemed the quickest path might at some point be seen as being too risky a gamble...

That reminds me of a story about an infamous boozer...the actor Richard Burton. *('Offer a warning' theme.)* When he died the doctors carried out an autopsy and found his entire internal organs were soaked and permeated with alcohol crystals. Thankfully that hasn't happened to you. With these understandings deeply embedded...

Safety feature module.

(WARNING: Alcohol withdrawal can ***kill*** *a heavy drinker! You must include a module somewhere in the session to ask the subconscious to cut down gradually in a 100% safe way. Usually this means the former drinker reduces their alcohol consumption over a few days to a week in my experience; it depends. The module that follows is taken from my book 'Wizards of trance' - it trusts that* ***the subconscious knows best,*** *because it does...)*

You need to ***cut down on your alcohol consumption*** at a safe rate and speed. Bit by bit, daily until you reach a moderate sensible, healthy level. You, the subconscious know this safe rate and speed and will only let this person reduce their alcohol consumption at this rate.

Future pace.

Phase 1: Watching objectively.

Like watching a movie of yourself over there... ***visualise*** a time when you would have drunk to excess in the past...when you would have used that old, outdated habit. That's it. BUT... See that you over there acting differently...in ways that prove ***that no longer bothers you...***See that you calm, relaxed confident and sober. See that you responding much more effectively. Handling all that comes their way with ***a greater sense of ease and humour.*** Know ***that person is free of alcohol, now.*** Know ***that person is beyond what was.*** Know ***that person is in control...***See how that you can ***feel so much better...***

What is it about the way they act and move that reveals ***that person is clearheaded and fully sober...*** (?) Watch them go through that situation in a new set of ways...That's it. I'll be quiet while to do that. *(Pause 20 seconds or so.)*

Phase 2: Associate into the 'best you'.

(In hypnosis we can trigger the brain's 'imitation impulse' – future rehearsal allows the person to imitate an imagined self who is 'well'. In hypnosis the brain believes that imagination is reality input – ah!) When ***you are happy*** with that...float into that experience from the beginning and go through it seeing it from your own point of view...See through those calm, sober, ***confident*** eyes! Hear through those ears that no longer listen to lies! Feel how wonderful it is to ***be fully in control of yourself, now.*** That's it.

Re-connect to your power! Re-connect to your sense of freedom! Re-connect to your 100% native ability to ***feel calm and relaxed...***Re-connect to you 100% native ability to ***feel good natural feelings naturally...***Re-connect to your very human ability to ***be behaviourally flexible...***If what you do isn't working ***act differently*** and get different results. Somehow you just ***become absorbed by these new ways...***Good.

Get a sense of knowing, with knowing feelings, that your health, wealth, relationships, finances and more are just improving tangibly. Go through that situation with the sense that there is ***no problem whatsoever.*** I'll be quiet for a full minute as you ***learn from your better***

self, unconsciously. *(NFH: Do so…)* Excellent! You are doing really well!

Ignoring messages.

(A key theme in hypnotic addiction work is 'ignoring the irrelevant'…)

When you ignore something, someone that tried to get your attention…when you ***refocus your attention*** on what *is* helpful, healthy and relevant for all parts of you, now…you'll find that they get the message and leave you well alone. ***Feel very powerful*** just knowing this reality.

Summation suggestions.

As the days and weeks and months progress… this progress only becomes more and more strongly entrenched throughout your mind and body…throughout your life. It's as though others notice that…***a new attractive energy radiates from you.*** And that sobering realisation only attracts better and better ways for you to ***get all of your genuine needs of any kind easily met*** in sensible ways on a daily basis.

When all the parts of you are pulling in the same direction…and they are, now…you'll find that ***staying off of alcohol is mysteriously***

easy....That the new way of life makes you ***feel alive and truly happy,*** down and up and through and about the core of who you truly deeply are...So that ***you can get on with the adventure of living...***

Going with the flow of change is fun...you never stop having problems...you just get better, more interesting ones...and you ***find better solutions*** to solve them. And that's that.

You will return with ***a feeling of clarity of mind and purpose. A feeling of calm*** unlike any you have any you have ever known. And this will, upon awakening, confirm to your conscious mind that...you have truly re-connected to who you really are deep inside. That amazing re-associations have occurred in a myriad of ways that will surprise and delight you. Your subconscious is always helping you...***ENJOY BEING SOBER!*** And it's nice to know that ***all this is so.'***

(I have never had a heavy drinker who wanted to stop altogether – I had 1 moderate drinking client who eventually went teetotal but that was it; but if a person wants to be teetotal just say that 'You are teetotal' etc. instead of saying 'You are a moderate drinker etc.' Identity level suggestions are powerful. The 'levels of mind are': behaviour, beliefs, identity, core. Actually they interrelate.)

Once more with feeling: there is no such thing as an 'addictive personality'.

I have written in other books about this – repeat after me class: THERE IS NO SUCH THING AS AN 'ADDICTIVE PERSONALITY'. That was made up by therapists and drug companies to get you hooked on therapy or drugs! Very simple. You need the right hypnotic interventions. You need to get your needs met. You need to fix your life. Do that and that pesky old 'addictive personality' turns into a healthy one: go figure!!!

If someone claims that such a bogus entity exists ask them to prove it with genetic research. They will have none carried out by anyone without monetary interests in keeping this toxic meme out there. And even the moneyed interests have no proof. Say something often enough via the media and people will believe it. Imagine a baby – do you really think it was BORN an addict??! Do try to think.

Case 6: The hateful yuppie gang of marijuana addicts!

What a bunch of degenerate scum they really were. A whole gang of London 'city boy' types ('finance industry' workers) called me to arrange a 'de-drugification' session. I only agreed to see them one at a time: what a sorry mess they were. All of them were stoners; they'd do their trading jobs by day and apart from the senior manager they'd blow almost all their cash on drugs – primarily cannabis. They'd get together after work and sit in some dingy or expensive flat/apartment depending on how the cash flow was and get stoned. All night. They would just watch TV and talk crap to eat other. This had become their degenerate lifestyle. And they loved it! But...

There were consequences – relationship trouble; if they had one! They were unable to function at all at work, they were becoming depressed. Their lives were stuck – in fact the whole office was in a mess. Putting my personal contempt (I loathe yuppies!) for these parasites aside I sought to help them. The trouble was when one relapsed the others fell too, like a house of cards. The manager was the linchpin. He was the only one with the brains to take a lead on the matter so I focused my attack on him. I also had to bear in mind that the London financial businesses are staffed by psychopaths and secondary psychopaths – this man lived and worked in a pathocratic environment: all back-stabbing and double-dealing, he could trust no one. Really his 'cure' was – get out of that profession fast. To cover all that I did would be impossible – in the end it took 4 sessions. Below is an example of one such session: unlike with the degenerate in question, a motivated normal client will benefit straight away. As with all other work: negotiation script 2 1st. Then...

Phase 1: Belief change NLPesque style.

(When dealing with addictions, remember the importance of the theme of 'belief'. This pattern can be immensely powerful – often with addictions the client lacks belief, one way or another that they can change, that freedom is possible. In that case you must address that reality if you are to successfully help a person escape the addiction parasite. The belief change required might be about perceptions that this person is a smoker or marijuana user – it has become an identity issue not a behavioural response to something. False though such a belief may be, you could do a ton of good change work but if the old belief is still working away unconsciously it might well screw everything else up, unless it spontaneously changes during hypnosis etc., which can happen. It is a straightforward 14

step procedure...)

1. **Identify the belief** - Okay: first we need to identity that belief that held you back up until now. Ask yourself, 'What I believe about myself is x,'...*(NFH: I am a junkie/smoker, pot head etc.)* So just locate that and know what it is to your satisfaction. I'll be quiet for a bit while you do that. *(Pause for 7-10 seconds etc.)*

2. **Meta belief check** - Good. Now, what do you believe about that old belief? Step back and ask yourself: what meanings and associations do you give it...Again I'll be quiet while you clarify that. *(Pause 10-15 seconds or so.)*

3. **Represent belief (NLP submodality work)** - Great. Now, notice how you represent that to yourself internally? Do you say something in a certain tone? With certain words? Do you feel something? Hear a sound? Smell a smell? Do you get an image? If so where is it in your mind's eye? How big is it? Is it colour or black and white? Is it far away? Close? Bright or dim etc.? Notice whatever comes to mind. Get to really know that way that you uniquely represent that belief to yourself

internally. I'll be quiet again. *(10-15 secs.)*

4. **Represent doubt** - Okay. As soon as you've finished...Imagine a white sheet of paper or something neutral and ***relax...***Fine. Next, think of something you doubt. What are its qualities? Again, notice how you represent that to yourself internally. Do you say something in a certain tone? Do you hear a sound? Do you feel something somewhere? Do you get an image and if so where is it exactly? Is it in a different place than the old belief image? How big is it? Colour or black and white? Far, away, close? Just notice whatever comes to mind automatically. Observe it. Be aware of all that. I'll be quiet again. *(10-15 secs.)*

5. **Note contrasts and differences** - Good. Imagine a white sheet of paper or something neutral and ***relax deeper***...Excellent. Now you've done that, notice how those things differ. Notice all of the contrasts between them. *(Allow about 10 secs – you don't have to keep saying, 'I'll be quiet now etc.'; after a few times they get the message.)*

6. **Experiment 1 (NLP submodality manipulation entrainment)** - Good. Imagine that sheet of white paper etc. again...Okay. Now take that thing you have believed up till now. Notice that way you represent that. What we are going to do now is experiment. I want you to notice any changes that occur to that belief when you deliberately alter its qualities. For example you can play around with the brightness, size, position; turn any sounds up or down, make them stereo or mono, does dimming effect it? Just play with that image for a while as if you were a film director. Feel free to play with it before we change it. Especially note – what enhances the belief and makes it stronger? *(Give them 30 secs.)*

7. **Experiment 2** – Okay. Good. Just ***relax*** and imagine something neutral. Just ***rest*** a moment...Fine. Now, you are going to experiment with changing the qualities of that doubt image etc. Just play around with its brightness, size, position; turn any sounds you like up or down - does dimming affect it? Play about with it – like a film director again and – notice the things that make the doubt stronger. Okay – just go ahead and do that. *(30 secs pause.)*

8. **New belief elicitation** – Good. Just ***relax deeply*** again. Imagine something nice and neutral...Okay: what belief would you like to have to ***replace that old limiting one, now,*** that stopped you from achieving this worthy goal? Could be, 'I am a non-smoker/non-marijuana user/free person etc. for the rest of my life.' Might be, 'I can really ***maintain this change.'*** Choose your new empowering belief now...State it in positive terms as an ability or process. Find an image that fully encapsulates that belief too. And notice all its qualities. *(Pause 20 secs or so.)*

9. **Ecology check** – And ***relax nicely*** once more. Good. Now, does any part of you object to this change? *(If you get any responses, and I never have, assure that part that its positive intentions will be taken into account – if needed, do a parts negotiation script from this book after you have completed this belief change work.)*

10. **Limiting belief into doubt** – Great! Think about that old, unhealthy, unwanted and most important unrealistic belief you had - now, *(say the next bit quickly)* quickly change that

representation into the exact qualities that doubt has instantaneously, that's right!

11. **Back and forth switch** – *(Continue with direct and faster tone)* Now quickly and several times change it back and forth, back and forth, faster and faster, back and forth, faster and faster from belief to doubt! Belief to doubt! Belief to doubt! Faster and faster and faster! Good – you might feel a bit disorientated or confused about it temporarily.

12. **Belief replacement** – Now quickly, turn all the sounds, brightness, colours, whatever down on that old negative belief image so that you can't even see, feel or hear it or its old affect/effect, in the past; it's gone, blacked out, whited out, whatever happens now. Switch your new better, healthier belief back and forth between the qualities of belief and doubt, several times – faster and faster!

13. **Final replacement (locking in)** – *(State firmly, quite a quick pace)* Put the new empowering belief in place fast! Now make sure finally, once and for all, that you change all the qualities of this new belief so that it looks and sounds

and feels etc. like something you totally believe in! ***It's a conviction! A part of your identity, now.*** Make those changes fast! Automatic! Lock them in and keep them! You've made it ***compelling real, now.***

14. **<u>Future pace</u>** – Just relax and go even deeper – 10 times deeper, feeling so relaxed and good. Now, consider what this looks, sounds like for you...imagine now, how ***this will affect your life positively.*** See it as a movie over there! ***You are living with this new belief,*** acting from it, experiencing from it! How much healthier do you look and feel? Experience all that vividly now! *(5-10 secs pause...)* Good! Now, when you are ready – step inside, drift or float into that movie and ***experience first-hand living and acting upon that healthy, better belief, now.*** That old belief isn't even an issue, wasn't it? See through those eyes, hear through those ears, feel how good it feels to ***fully own that belief, now.*** That's it! You are doing brilliantly. Now let's start to do some things to ***end that marijuana habit.***

Phase 2: Dissociate from old habits – associate into the new.

Before we continue it's 100% necessary that you are honest with yourself...You now ***know that marijuana is a thieving, abusive parasite*** – knowing this you can ***stop believing its lies!*** With that reality firmly embedded in your deepest mind, now...

Step 1: Dissociate from an old pattern.

Recall a time when you had believed the propaganda of that drug...a time when you were just about to take it...And instantly – float out of that time and see that you over there... *(NFH: A key theme of this book is – hypnotically dissociate at the point where the client would have taken the drug; you might call this the 'urge point'. It is actually the moment the 'drug trance' kicks in.)* but you aren't doing what you normally did...The great thing is in hypnosis you can ***see alternatives...***

So imagine seeing that you over there doing something different in that situation....That's it. That you is ***calm, relaxed, confident and strong in that situation.*** If you always did what you've always done, you'll always get what you always got! So ***act and feel differently from now on.*** See that you doing something, healthy, fun, sensible...Perhaps something that satisfies a genuine need. That's right...You have a powerful will. You ***have a mind of your own.*** You have deep sources of organic motivation that propel you toward health, now. Everyone can ***think for yourself...*** *(I know it's not grammatically correct; it's not supposed to be!)* I'll be quiet for a bit to let you absorb the learnings of that experience. *(Pause for 7-10 secs only.)*

Step 2: Associate into new choices.

Good! Now, when you're ready – Float/drift inside that you who can ***easily behave and feel in the new ways...***See through those eyes that ***can see clearly, now...***Hear through those ears that ***ignore lies and false promises...***

Feel the confidence! Feel the pride! Feel the healthful feelings spreading all through you! Ah! ***Feel that mental clarity*** anyone can get when viewing a beautiful natural scene... You can do things that ***move your life forward...***in all the ways it's meant to...It's time to ***leave that junk behind and move on, now...***I'll be quiet as you ***feel free again...***to process this information appropriately. *(20 secs pause.)* Fine.

(You might want to repeat the 'dissociate and associate pattern' above up to 3 times using different past situations: it's your choice. It can only help. The more you rehearse something – the more ingrained it becomes but don't overdo it; the brain learns very quickly when motivated.)

Step 3: Future pace.

Like watching a movie of yourself – visualise a time in your future that will confirm ***this has really worked...***View yourself going through an entire 24 hour period...knowing, with knowing feelings inside, that that you is...***free of marijuana forever, now.***

Really enjoy the experience of seeing that you who...looks different...dresses differently...acts differently...feels differently...thinks differently... believes differently... *(all 'levels' of the personality covered)* is a different person... ***Unable to go into that old drug trance, now.*** Lives differently in more ways than one... Good...Recognise these changes that occurred, didn't you?

As you go through this time...know that in the 20 seconds that follow you can experience a whole day of freedom...because in trance, time is flexible...*(Wait 20 secs.)*

<u>*Associate into the new patterns.*</u>

Good. You are doing very good work. Now, imagine floating into that future time of ***success, now...***From beginning to end... ***feeling free from the inside out!*** Look through the ***experience - being free.*** Hear through the ears of freedom and health! ***Feel amazing*** as you know, really know...that you can...***permanently break free from that old pattern, unconsciously, now...***Again I'll be quiet for about 20 seconds...And that's enough time inside to ***go through a whole day of freedom...*** *(Pause 20 secs.)*

You are a non-smoker, not an ex-smoker, a non-smoker...And ***this is your true identity*** at the deepest levels of experience, is it not? Will you not? Haven't you? Non-smokers find that at certain times...when needed...automatically... ***thoughts and feelings and hopes and ideas that fully support this change will just be there...***And that a nice thing to know, isn't it. Your subconscious will assist you in all your efforts for its own reasons. All appropriate parts of you will appropriately help.

You can stubbornly stay on this healthy path. You can ***successfully rebel against the tyranny of any drug...***There are things you will and won't do...and those things have changed, altered, profoundly, healthily, wisely, now...

Your creative part generates new choices with positive intent that lead to very real satisfactions that make ***you feel so naturally good.***

Your ***inner strength is firm and resolved to win!*** As we mature we learn that there are ***better ways to respond to the challenges of life,*** do we not, have you not? Didn't you? You have a strong sense of enduring determination to ***stay free and happily healthy,*** now...and this is so.

Phase 3: Take care of free time.

(When people take drugs they waste a lot of time – when they stop they have more free time to kill – get them imagining what enjoyable stuff they'll do instead.)

Step 1: Dissociate.

Imagine as a movie goer again – a great variety of things you would genuinely like to do...Now that you ***put the past unwanted patterns far behind you...***You have so much more time...Imagine the activities you'll enjoy doing from now on...Exercise? Learning new skills? Reading? Socialising? Dating etc.? *(Obviously suit to the client's needs.)* Anything and everything that helps you ***meet genuine emotional, physical and psychological needs naturally from this moment on.***

Essentially you are practising having a real life that is healthily fun to live! You feel so much more lively! Take a whole minute to rehearse that, in the pause... *(Wait for 1 minute.)* Very good x...*(x = client's name; see 'How to hypnotise anyone' for details of name use.)*

Step 2: Associate.

Now float into those experiences...try out as many as you like...find which choices suit you best and when...And see and hear and sense and touch and taste and most importantly ***feel how much better those new ways are*** and remember to ***commit to this positive change with all your heart and soul, noooo-oooooow!*** That's it!

(Quiet for a full minute! Remember success with stopping any unwanted habit, in part, entails dissociating from completing it in the imagination at the point of the initiation of old triggers and associating into healthier patterns – this sends a signal to the subconscious: not that – this!)

Soon, very soon I'll show you a way to ***feel good without artificial aids...****so that you* *can* ***break free from that old loop...*** With that very real reward in mind, let's continue... *(This creates positive expectancy!)*

Phase 4: Fast-forward to the consequences manoeuvre.

(This is like the scrooge pattern – a reality check. Junkies etc. kid themselves – they are operating from a Gnostic fantasy. Some say to me – 'I wish I could do the drug and not have the bad effects.' This is like saying I wish I could jump out of a ten storey building and bounce! NEVER GOING TO HAPPEN. Be more diplomatic in reality obviously. Gnostic thinking patterns unconsciously affect many people: the West has been infiltrated by them – they are an information disease; for more on this see book 7, 'Escaping cultural hypnosis.' I actually developed this pattern after having a client who told me to make her hate puff/cannabis. I didn't listen to her and failed her. 'Time distortion' is a major theme of addiction busting protocols...)

To really ***reinforce these changes*** let's do some things to solidify things beautifully. Okay... next...recall or imagine a time just before you were about to use x *(cannabis etc.)*...Good... Notice any internal responses you are having... Notice the external environment...Now, instantaneously – very quickly fast-forward in time till afterwards when you ***feel those horrible feelings of regret again...***What a mistake that was and you know it. That's a genuine feeling. A wise feeling – learn from it unconsciously, now. *(Pause a beat – 5 secs max.)*

I want you to go through that experience again...Recall or conjure up a time you were about to do x...Good...Notice any internal responses you are having...Notice the external environment...Now, instantaneously – very quickly fast-forward in time till afterwards when you feel those horrible feelings of regret again... ZIP! What a mistake that was and you know it. That's a genuine feeling. Double those unpleasant feelings...A wise feeling – ***learn from it...unconsciously, now.*** *(Allow 5 secs or so processing time.)*

I want you to go through that experience again...one more time for luck...Visualise a time you were about to do x...Good...Notice any internal responses you are having...Notice the external environment...Now, instantaneously – very quickly fast-forward in time till afterwards when you feel those horrible feelings of regret again...ZAP! What a mistake that was and you know it. That's a genuine feeling. And that feeling feels worse this time...Triple that unpleasant feeling...A wise feeling – learn from it unconsciously, now. Very good...

And these unpleasant feelings can teach you... in your own way that ***old urges fade away completely, without knowing how, didn't you?*** And if you were EVER to seriously consider to even ***try in vain*** to go back to the old ways...that old illusory, lying feeling of excitement and anticipation...will be utterly smothered by this feeling of regret...to an appropriate degree by your deepest unconscious...because you need to ***learn certain lessons...***Before you made less than wise choices, than what's beyond that, wasn't it?

If you were to temporarily consider back-sliding...automatically highly dissuasive thoughts and images of the negative results of using x *(drug etc.)* will pop into your mind...This is a post...hypnotic...command, now! *(Say with authority!)*

All actions have un-evadable consequences for good or ill...your deepest awareness is fully in tune with this reality, now. But the good thing is when you ***choose to stay on a healthy path*** each time you ***do that...***your emotive mind will reward you with a very pleasant feeling...

(Readers of my earlier books may have noticed I say that it is best NOT to use 'negative' associations in trance work. BUT if the client is associating to perceived 'good associations' that

are drug induced and objectively false you have got to address that. People who don't use drugs think of all the bad results – this is what keeps them clean. With an addict you are teaching them how to respond normally – in such cases 'negative' but skilled use of N.A.C is permissible. With this manoeuvre you are utilising 2 aspects of what hypnosis does best – <u>refocusing and amplification.</u> Notice I also throw in a reward feeling for being sensible – 'conditioning with pleasure' as it's called. I take the old strategy: ***trigger/urge - excitement – drug – regret/pain*** *and replace it with:* ***trigger/urge - doubt/regret – healthy new choice – pleasure!*** *A so-called 'trigger' ALWAYS emerges as a result of various unmet needs. Our instincts demand satisfaction!)*

<u>Phase 5: Resist the drug trap – Greek metaphors and more!</u>

(My yuppie junkie could not resist temptation or control that drug urge when he was with a group of friends: even a 'think for yourself' module failed. That being so I had to leave any anti group-think strategy and build in some inner strength. Next I show you how – specifically...)

Seduction – means 'to be led astray'. It sounds nice but...there are short, medium and long term consequences to all we do...and when

you are calm and you can think straight, now...you can consider such things with clarity.

That reminds me about the story of Odysseus and the Sirens...Odysseus was an adventurer... He loved to take risks, experiment and explore...On his journeys he came to the Island of the Sirens...The Sirens were mythical creatures – monsters really...their top half was beautiful: they had the torso, face, hair, arms and bare breasts of the most beautiful women you could ever meet...They were much more tantalising and attractive than any mortal women could dream of being...but the reality was their bottom half was that of a ravenous bird of prey...They had sharp claws...and hidden in their pretty mouths were fangs for eating human flesh...

The thing about them was that no mortal man could ***resist*** their singing...It was no use telling that ***inner voice of temptation - be silent!*** No, no, no – the siren song was too alluring...it promised immediate pleasures beyond worldly imaginings...The appeal of that song was *too* appealing...Men had been known to become so overwhelmed with desire in those past times... that they jumped overboard – the emotional brain had swamped their thinking part...the part that allows you to ***calmly think through the consequences of actions...***

Now, Odysseus was a sea captain...He ordered his crew – the team that backed up his decisions...to tie him fast to the boat's mast... and once he was firmly tied so that he could not move...the crew bunged/filled up their ears with wax so that...***that part of the team couldn't hear that voice of temptation...***And even though the Sirens sang...and even though Odysseus heard their singing and begged and pleaded and demanded to be released...***that old message can't get through*** if the crew hears no noise from the captain... *(Confusion: who or what is the captain? Don't worry the subconscious will make sense of it...)* Because on any important journey we pass a point of no return...and as his ship passed by the island of the Sirens...those old deceptively alluring voices grew quieter and quieter....and at a certain point...as things are in flux...***old feelings have diminished considerably...***

With that deeply embedded in your mind now... we can continue...I would like to speak to the emotive part of you...This is the part of you that had overwhelmed you with an impulse in the past...I would like to thank that part for doing what it did so well...I would like it to know that I know that it was doing its best to help you... but as we get older and ***mature...***we all learn, really learn how to ***control your emotions*** and so...for your own reasons as a whole person...***lower that level of unnecessary,***

counterproductive arousal, unconsciously now...Because it is the higher part of your brain – your captain if you like...who can make really good decisions when ***you remain calm in situations that once troubled you...*** wasn't it? Because when you ***feel so much calmer overall from now on...***you can know that it's been proven scientifically that people can...***ignore temptation...***The front part of your brain starts to take control over waking life much more and more once we get passed our teens...it learns to ***consider consequences in the now...in the medium term and in the long term...***

Symbology/personification of temptation/impulse etc.

Can you conjure some symbol, perhaps a personification of what a confidence trickster looks like to you? That's it...Notice the colours... Any noises...Any smells...The location...The lighting...Notice any feelings of distrust and disgust that you instinctively feel to anything a character like that might say...like a voice you simply do not believe...and...***you do not believe that lying voice any-more...***

You know that it is a deceiver at a very deep level of awareness, now...You don't listen to its siren song...you don't listen to its lies...you know all ***that was a con...***Consider now how it had actually promised you the world and honestly delivered nothing it promised...just regrets...ill health...a lack of control...You felt enslaved with less money did you not? How much of your time did that con-man waste? Which relationships were harmed? And to what degree? What did you miss out on?

Friend image comparison.

If it helps, conjure up the image of a friend... That's it. *(Allow 3-5 secs...)* Someone who respects you, loves you...someone who would never misuse their influence...

And at a deep level – ***recognise the difference between the two, now.*** Very – good! Relax deeply and imagine a neutral image...

Boost self-control.

Isn't it time to ***feel in control again...*** (?) That's right! Every team needs a captain – you might call that part 'Inner Strength'...Some call it the 'Leadership part'...we all know what is broadly meant...

There is a part built into you which must consider things from a mature perspective...***the part that is in executive control must lead...***must make the decisions...must ***define***

your will using your inherent power...just as a country needs a wise leader and can't be pushed around by the emotionalism of the unthinking mob!

The back of your mind...the part that had initiated that over arousal of the former times in those former ways can ***relax right now...*** because it had a positive function...It was only trying to make you ***feel good naturally...***but it was racing to act...and sometimes we need to ***slow certain processes down at certain times...***to ***act wisely,*** do we not? Will you not? Will you not? Haven't you? But when you **get your emotional, physical and psychological needs met on a daily basis** more and more and more...***the outdated signals from that part dampen down, all - the - way – down, now...***

Re-associate to strengths and install trigger.

(The following trigger gives an 'after care' prompt to dampen stressful trigger feelings that often lead to stupid risk taking.)

Can you recall a time you felt so calm, relaxed and in control...Good...Be in that time...see what you saw...hear what you heard...feel how good that ***calmness*** felt. Take that feeling of total calm and turn it into a colour...Let that soak through all of you...***Soak in the serenity...***

Now imagine the colour of that serenity only changing in ways that make ***this relaxing feeling, stronger and more intense...*** Excellent...Now say a trigger word that you associate with this state. Whenever you need to ***feel this state in your future...***you merely say your trigger word and it is there and you may find ***it's there anyway...***This is a post hypnotic command...

As you ***fully re-experience that state...*** you know from this place you make good decisions...you know from this place that ***you have ideals and values*** that you want to live up to more and more and more...That ***you are about far more than that,*** are you not? You have hopes and dreams and healthy yet fun desires that can be reconnected to now at a very fundamental level...Somehow you ***process certain information differently...***Somehow when you take risks – you ***take calculated risks*** that move you forward and give you a ***genuine feeling of reward and satisfaction...***

Now...spontaneity is not the same as impulsiveness. One is desirable and attractive - the other is as unnecessary as continuing to wear nappies/diapers... *(key theme of 'maturing')* we all ***outgrow certain things...*** It's nice to know, is it not, that...you can ***regain full mastery over yourself...*** *(? – this* *denotes a pseudo question...)* and the subconscious will aid you powerfully in all your endeavours...

Future pace.

(Re-associate and smoother old tensions etc.)

As though watching a movie: can you see a past you over there...in a time and place where you might have acted as you don't anymore (?) ...That you might be just starting to get a bit agitated and aroused...And from this calm place...and before they act...simply float into them ***calmly...***Let that you absorb all these positive learnings...let them spread and fill you...Notice your colour of calm fill you as you say your ***calming*** trigger word...head to toe... so that ***the old arousal is soothed away completely by this tranquil calm, now...***If it helps: imagine ***that old emotion is being replaced by the soothing, gentle colour of serenity...***Per-fect!

And notice as a result...***all those old feelings and responses somehow change and shift, unconsciously, now...***You ***feel a real sense of peace of mind and control...***Feel that 'the real captain' is in charge of the crew... feel a resolute conviction that whatever needs to finally adjust now to...***solidify these new understandings*** can do so without effort...

I will be quiet for a whole minute and in that time...your time...observe and then float into two more times when you might of acted how you don't...And feel how it feels to ***respond maturely...***to be able to ***think calmly and rationally in certain situations*** in which you once lacked that ability, in the past...Good. Go ahead and privately do that in your own way... *(Therapeutic theme of 'client privacy' – I need know nothing or little...Wait for 1 minute...)*

That's it. And you can take this act as a sign and a signal that...***you can resist any passing temptation or impulse...***it's just what you do...The old ways have faded, melted away...they no longer bother you in any way, shape or form and this is so...

You are calmly in control. You can think things through wisely. You are the boss of you. You ignore the unimportant. You turn away from deception. You can build a better life from your own efforts...You instinctively absorb all these new learnings... And there is a good feeling in knowing this to be true.

Great! Say to yourself, with feeling, once and for all – 'I am a happy and healthy person now. I am fully in control and it feels great!' Your calming trigger word is always there when you need it, you have knowing feelings that ***your***

sense of calmness is restored, now...

Phase 6: It's raining colour feelings! Build in good feelings without drugs.

(Druggies etc. must be retaught how to feel good again – naturally. So...)

Just ***visualise*** something neutral for a moment – good! Imagine you are in a beautiful place where it rains colours...And these colours are actually symbolic representations of all the natural good feelings that you could feel in a lifetime and to varying intensities...Not yet but soon I want you to stand under one of those colour-feelings that is raining down from that inner sky...And when you do, and when that wonderful colour feeling touches you...you will ***effortlessly absorb that feeling and feel it spreading*** all the way through your mind, body and soul...getting better, better, even better!

Okay, we'll do this 3 times with 3 different feelings...The cue word for you to catch a good feeling as it were is – *'Plentiful!'* Why? Because you unconsciously ***have plentiful amounts of good feeling within you*** without any external aids...That is your birth right. How you were 'designed' for want of a better word. I don't know what these good feelings will be...you don't know either...Your deepest mind does, trust its wisdom to help you ***feel the best you***

can, now... Got that? Ready? *(Rhetorical – don't wait!)* Here we go! 'Plentiful!'

Feel that amazing feeling spread all the way through you...making ***you feel glorious!*** Allow yourself to absorb that...***Feel its intensity grow!*** Perhaps that colour gets brighter somehow as it spreads all through you... (?) Filling you up with vast and unending reservoirs of ***natural good feelings, now...*** These feelings are those healthy ones you get when...you spend time with dear friends or relatives...eat good food...view nature...connect meaningfully with others! ***Feel so absorbed*** as you are when in the zone when everything just flows for you! And whatever else your subconscious processes believe is right for you to re-connect to.

Good. And once again you are going to stand under another of those lovely colour feelings. Here it comes! Get ready! 'Plentiful!' That's right! All the way through to the core of who you deeply, truly are and can be – again! Feel these feeling naturally intensify! Better, better, even better!

That's perfect! You are relearning that ***feeling good naturally is a part of your core identity, now.*** So ***old urges and desires for the unnatural just fade, melt away***

completely...Because the unconscious knows just what shifts to make in how you process information differently, unconsciously...Bathe and soak up the glow of these good feelings you possess within!

And one last time for luck...spot a falling colour feeling...one that looks particularly inviting and juicy! Get ready to stand beneath it. ***Make any final, necessary adjustments, now...***Here it comes! *(Build up the expectation!)* Feel that wonderful sense of anticipation that you get when you deserve a reward! *'Plentiful!'* Feel them soothe away any old, ***doubts or worries in the past...Feel the clarity! Feel the joy!*** Feel that ***peace of mind returned...***

In this state you ***make good decisions...***In this state you ***feel more positive and optimistic about so many things!*** In this state you ***powerfully reclaim your life!*** You cannot be bullied by lies here! Parasites have no power here! The ***power and control now lies deep within you.*** And that's a nice thing to know, isn't it? So you can ***enjoy the revivified experience of an abundance of good feelings within daily...***And as such – you can take this act as a sign and a signal... that you fully trust the wisdom of your emotive mind to allow you to ***experience better***

states of mind and body...Just the right level...of certain good feelings...remain with you. The outcome of so many changes is that you will...***feel fully alive again, nooooooooooow!*** And that's that. *(Pause a beat.)*

Now, just allow those images to wash away as you...***go 10 times more deeply into a relaxing hypnotic trance...***in your own manner...

Phase 7: Imagine a time in the future when the problem is far behind you.

You are doing great! We are almost done...Okay just allow this present time to fade away as you imagine being somewhere, at some time that has deep sets of associations to beauty, nature and ***a positive future for you...now...***Could be a woodland scene, mountain, beach – up to you...And as you get the sense of that personal place...know that it is five years into your future...Really imagine that vividly as through it's realistically lifelike and totally convincing...Good.

On a day like this you ***feel so glad to be alive...***You like living this life of yours. Every day contains new delights to discover...And not right now but soon enough I will click my fingers/say the word 'rose'...and when I do you will feel with 100% certainty that you are in that place...vividly, clearly, naturally and it fee-eels great – just soak in that experience...Notice the weather, light, sounds, smells, tastes...Take in, ***focus intently*** on all the mesmerising details that you find there...Good... *(FINGER CLICK! 'Rose!')*

Really listen to those natural healing sounds... attune yourself into the ***changing patterns*** of life...the rhythms of change...the reality of it. Imagine that and ***feel that*** you have had 5 whole years of being free of x *(drug etc.)* *(NFH: This is a very powerful module – I generally throw it in when I feel all work is done and we need to underline that the work is finished; it's time to move on!)* Experience the feel of comforting temperatures there...hear any relaxing sounds...feel those wonderful feelings... immerse yourself in the hypnotic reality of being there.

You have years and years of ***feeling that problem far behind you.*** You have years and years of just ***feeling confidently free...***your whole mind and body feels purified, clean and clear...you ***feel yourself glowing with glorious health...***Because it has been SO long ago since you last had/did x *(old response)*. Now ***you are resolved to remain free of that for good.*** That's it.

You feel, think and know this in that place

within where you are absolutely certain about certain matters inside...You can just sit there musing on this amazing new state of affairs... You can ***feel blissful feelings of pride, achievement, accomplishment...***and they will remain with you.

Such warm feelings well up within...they are spreading all throughout your being... intensifying and amplifying appropriately...their strength only continues to grow...And you can reflect in trance...how truly happy you are knowing that ***you have gotten rid of that old response...***so long ago.

As you continue the process, aware that ***you have stopped that now...***The feelings of bliss and joy only grow – getting stronger and stronger! With the momentum of some unstoppable force! And very soon...not now but in a moment, you'll be ***feeling all the joy you can contain.*** And become super aware that this is a sign and a signal of your ongoing success, unconsciously, now.

And when I awaken you later you'll ***bring all these good feelings,*** apart from the hypnotic trance obviously ***back with you into waking life.*** And as you know, really know...from experiential learning...that you are able to ***feel good now,*** feel good tomorrow...and on and on and on...As good as you will feel in fact...

with the recognition that...***you have achieved that goal,*** wasn't it? You ***feel so calm and confident*** pretty much all the time...The old ways have faded away, melted away, now...so only ***honest pride and joy is present*** in response...Such deep satisfaction emerges within, now...Happiness and natural thrills result...such a sense of inspired stimulation results – You have accomplished that which you sought and you just know it at very deep levels of information processing. Good.

You will find spontaneously that your mind is simply filled with good reasons why you are happy that you did what you've done...So happy you stopped the old response...replaced with ***super-abundant energetic confidence*** and more! You ***desire to carry on in this manner...***maintaining this goal of ***remaining a non-smoker/drug free/teetotal etc. for the rest of your long and healthy life, now...***And that's nice to know, isn't it?

Okay you've done brilliantly – time to wrap up! Bring your sense of time and place back to here now...Before I begin to begin the process of... ***you're starting to wake up...***back to now but still somewhat entranced and comfortable... It was not so much the how, the mechanics and the what not...but the fact that you have stopped what you once did and started ***living free and confidently, now,*** that was of significance...***Feel a sense of peace and completion*** that you will bring back with you... And those knowing feelings confirm...it's done.'

(The above is a long and fancy 'future pace' I use when I feel 'closure' – that vile word – is at hand. Start exduction proper next etc. That should sort a motivated client out. I often simply bombard a client's subconscious into submission. It works!)

Helpful trick bonus: gaining authority, prestige and rapport through 'deep understanding'.

There is a sure fire way to gain trust quickly – demonstrate wisdom and understanding to your client that you **recognise his or her needs and the reality of their life.** How do you do it? Real easy and simple.

- A client says they are worried about quitting a hateful job. Assure them that you know that financial realities must be taken into consideration.
- A client says he fears working alone. Ask him if not socialising so much will be a problem?
- A client comes from a background where ambition was not encouraged. Say – people from certain backgrounds are just trying to protect you the best way they know how etc.

What are you doing? Like a 'psychic' cold reader you are showing you get their situation; that their very real concerns are normal and understood. You can be precise or vague and cut to the gist of what they're tentatively trying to admit or face up to. When you do it well and come across *really* insightful they'll say, 'You just really crystallised/raised someone important there etc.'

Ask: what is the underlying need of this person in this situation? If people talk around a point as if trying to reach an understanding – clarify it for them accurately. This is when you start coming across as Yoda! Almost as if you are 'mind-reading'; you aren't, you just understand people.

Case 7: Candy is quicker – sugar/chocolate addiction ain't so sweet!

The 'presenting problem' was sugar addiction. The real problem matrix (see book 3, 'Powerful hypnosis' for the full definition) I identified was:

- **Sugar addiction.** See the script included here.
- **Habitual background worry.** So severe that he couldn't enjoy life.
- **Emotional eating.** I had to decouple unmet needs from hunger signals.
- **Terror of being independent.** This man wanted to quit an old job and start his own business – this thought was so terrifying to him I had to de-traumatise him! See book 9, 'Hypnotically annihilating anxiety' for the process.
- **Inability to feel sufficient pleasure in daily life.** I used the 'Peak of ultimate bliss script!' from crafting hypnotic spells to teach him to how to feel good even if he wasn't achieving goals. It amazes me how so many people, especially men will not feel good until a specific goal is achieved; enjoy the process of living for God's

sake!

- **Extreme work stress and tension.** Privatisation in his workplace was leading to a form of Orwellian bullying that was taking its toll physically and mentally. He had just avoided a full 'nervous breakdown'.

- **Conscious suppression of genuine life goals and instinctive drives.** Denying one's own deepest seated desires through fear and so developing a whole host of psychosomatic problems as the unconscious desperately tried to communicate with consciousness about its displeasure.

- **'Working class' social programming.** Being brainwashed that 'people like us' don't do certain things 'above our station'. Really! What is this, the Middle- Ages???! To a certain extent yes! We live in Neo-feudal times.

- **Very mild O.C.D (Obsessive Compulsive Disorder patterns).** The simple fact of going to school on his own as a small boy and the stress involved had led to small rituals to allay fears and worries (see book 7, 'Escaping cultural hypnosis' on the unnatural rite of state/public school education). They were very mild – once old worrying patterns were diminished to sensible levels and a suggestion to stop doing the old rituals was given – they vanished.

A problem matrix is just the constellation of interrelated parts that = the 'presenting problem' in reality. Every client's problem matrix is subtly different. This whole process took 4 sessions – because I can't physically talk that long in one go! My head would explode!

As we are just focusing on the pure addictive processes in this book, here is your sugar/chocolate etc. addiction deprogramming script. Here's a tip – you can have TOO much of a good thing. Use that.

Controlling sugar intake script.

(This can also be used with weight loss clients. Often overeating is a form of addiction anyway. If you recall, I have used parts negotiation with weight loss clients with great success.)

Step 1: Changing tastes preamble/proem.

(The following is a deft example of good Neuro-Associative-Conditioning: 'N.A.C'...)

'Life is a funny thing because ***your tastes change. Now...*** we don't even have to know the how of how that happened, wasn't it? But it can and does happen to lots of people...I couldn't stand the taste of olives, ***as a child.*** And now, as an adult I LOVE olives...It's like that person you had that crush on when you were younger...and then somehow, ***some process of change can take place...***whereby that which was attractive, isn't anymore...Not that you dislike it...you just ***like it less...***and ***less often too...***And have you heard that saying, 'He or she is TOO nice...'? Well chocolate/biscuits/sweets/candy etc. can be like that...because the fact is we aren't supposed to eat that much refined white sugar...in fact it's entirely new in our diet as humans...it causes tooth decay, weight gain; it can even lead to diabetes if consumed to excess...

Here you can ***consider the consequences*** of certain old patterns... *(key theme: 'consequences'!)* The fact is that by and large sugary foods have very little if any nutritional value...You don't need what they have in order to survive...but it was like that sugar had tricked your mind into focusing on it rather than all the other amazing, wide ranging types of food that there really are available...So many other foodstuffs on earth that you can ***refocus your mind*** toward, ***now.***

What other food would you like to try? Any diet that stays the same quickly becomes deadly dull. Would you like chocolate etc. so much if you just ate that all day, day in, day out? ***That kind of routine can become boring,*** can't it? And you need genuine stimulation, variety and choice to ***get your genuine nutritional needs met,*** in your own unique way... Sometimes that just happens as you ***become more indifferent to certain things...***

Step 2: Too much sugar visualisation.

Phase 1: Dissociative observation of old pattern.

(Goal – to create realistic objectivity.)

What if you could use that powerful brain of yours to visualise a you over there, eating too much sugary stuff...Look at that you stuffing their face with all those cakes, biscuits/cookies, chocolate bars...all those sugary foods...What does that look like to see a table piled up and up...over the top with heaps of sugary stuff? Does that you look particularly dignified? Does that you look genuinely happy with their lot?

What if that you not only starts stuffing their face with all those sugary cakes but that they have a pot of sticky treacle, caster/icing/powdered/confectioner's sugar etc.

and white refined sugar in large pots nearby… and so much does that you lust after sugar that they start to use a large spoon and they begin to ladle the treacle etc. all over the cakes and biscuits and chocolate – YUCK!

And they aren't satisfied with that! Then they use the biggest spoon they can find and they cover all those sugary foods with spoonfuls of the sweetest castor and refined sugar they can find. If they had a tub of any kind of syrup they'd add all that too!

Imagine that scene vividly…see all that sugar and treacle around their mouth and all over their hands – YUCK! Is that in any way an appetising prospect? Really? What is all the sugar doing to that person's body? What is it doing to raise their blood sugar levels? What damage are they doing to their teeth? How much weight might they gain?

(When asking questions in trance leave enough processing time, however the subconscious can multi-task; it can process multiple information processing subroutines at once…)

And the thing is they are eating so quickly they aren't really paying attention to the overly sickly taste of too much sugar…Almost like they were hypnotised, in a trance while eating…

Phase 2: Associate into extreme sugar binging.

Well it's time that ***you are fully conscious of your taste buds' response while eating...*** So in order to never do what that imaginary you was doing...imagine drifting into that imaginary you and really ***tasting the sickly sweet taste of too much sugar...***Feel how uncomfortable it feels in your mouth...Urgh! *(Use a voice tone of disgust!)* All that sugar! It just tastes TOO sweet! It's sickly sweet! You really can have too much of a good thing and it's time to ***stop that, now.*** Imagine eating more and more...it's just ***TOO sweet and sugary!*** Focus in on the sensations of ***too much icky sticky sugar... too sweet for you...too many biscuits/cookies...too many cakes...too much candy...***As you ***fully experience that unpleasant sensation*** you can double it! Double it again!

Feel how sickly too much sugar really tastes and take that learning with you, now... Magnify that sensation one last time so that ***at that level it just tastes too sickly sweet,*** does it not?!

Now, as you begin to pay attention to your body's genuine responses you can take this act as a sign and a signal that you can ***moderate your sugar intake daily...***All children know when they are full, when they've had enough of anything...and ***you can re-associate to that native ability*** you have always had...

Now, the good thing is that imaginary time never really happened...You can drift out of that you...taste buds fully back to normal but with that learning and understanding of ***sensible limits in place, unconsciously.*** That's right.

Step 3: Direct negotiation and suggestions.

You don't need to stop eating treats every now and again...A treat is a treat because ***you don't do it too often...old desires and urges can naturally diminish...***new associations can smoother old ones...healthier options are available...With that in mind, know that I am still speaking to your other mind... what some people call the subconscious or ***you're/your deeply unconscious, now...***Up to this point in life you had been responding in certain ways...eating far too much of that which you didn't need...and I know you had very good reasons for that...I know your intent was positive – whatever that was: *(key theme: 'positive intent'!)* ***honour the intent by making healthier choices, now...***

I know you understand and appreciate that what is the optimum response now is to ***greatly diminish this person's sugar intake...***You don't fill a car with petrol/gas till it flows out of the petrol/gas tank...that costs money...There is a price to pay and over time it could be genuinely dangerous...

The best thing now is to ***eat what your body truly desires to stay fit and healthy...*** Signals can bubble up to consciousness suggesting this and that food to ***eat nutritiously, from now on...***Maybe images... urges for certain foods which contain what your mind and body really needs...because you do need some sugar in your diet...your brain needs it to function...glucose is brain fuel...but there are better types of sugar and better ways of getting it...

And you – the part of this person that is responsible for their appetites can ***make any and all appropriate changes now,*** so that this person controls their sugar intake...so they can...***eat sensibly...get emotional needs met...get physical needs met...get psychological needs met...get relationship needs met...achieve worthy goals...***and ***derive satisfaction from the process of living...***Thaa-aat's it.

Step 4: Future pace to lock in changes.

Phase 1: Dissociated observation.

With these lessons in living in mind, imagine

now...a healthy you at some time in your brighter, happier future who is ***in control now...***they can be eating at any time of day that confirms ***this has worked powerfully!*** See the healthy food they are enjoyably eating. See how much better they look in mind and body? ***Fitter, more clarity of mind: taste buds tastes altered appropriately, now...*** Great!

Imagine someone offers them a sugary treat and the new you can either ***pleasantly decline it*** or ***eat just the right amount then stop.*** Each and both are fine. There are always more than one set of responses...more than one way to overcome any obstacle...***being calm and creative*** helps...

See how relaxed and confident that you is...How they respond to others and life differently...See how that you can ***feel so differently about sugar*** in general...***attitudes can change...***I'll be quiet for a full 30 seconds while you imagine that... *(Do so...)*

Phase 2: Associated new experience imprinting.

Okay, now – to really ***lock in and solidify these amazing changes***...go through the experience from the inside...Go back to the beginning of that scene and see it from your point of view...Float, ***drift*** into the new you...

experience the new responses from the inside...Look through those eyes of you in control! Hear through those ears! Notice the new sensations inside – indifference, enough is enough, new urges and whatever else had changed for the better...Appropriate images, perhaps, that make you ***act differently in those situations...***And most importantly grasp how that makes you ***feel differently too...*** automatically...***Feel that sense of self-control and power...Feel healthier...Feel your clarity of mind and purpose...Feel so calm and confident...***And blend them together doubly so...And feel these wonderful feelings radiate from you! And that feels really good doesn't it? Keep them as a gift to yourself. Again I will be quiet for a whole minute this time as you ***process that meaningfully...***

End metaphor and wrap up.

The river flows ever onward...The twig gets caught and snagged temporarily before the flow of things takes them downstream again on the inevitable progress of anyone's experience... That's it. You have unlearned what you had learned, wasn't it? ***Trust your subconscious*** to aid you in many empowering ways...in all your much better choices. And this is so. The process is complete and you sense it... feelingly...now.'

(Lob in a wake up or attack another part of the problem matrix etc. Note: what I have provided above is but 1 option; the alternatives are countless.)

Random useful modules bonus.

I include here some useful random metaphors/symbology work that a therapist/hypnotist/hypnotherapist can use or add to the other modules in this book. I have used 'em all – at the right time and place, and using your judgement as to appropriateness, they all work. Obviously deep hypnosis is required first.

Metaphor 1: Outgrowing old relationships.

(There is a time in life when we all outgrow old friends. When we realise that certain relationships aren't productive or healthy and that we need to move on: in that case try the metaphor that follows...key theme: 'abusive relationships'.)

Moving on metaphor.

Step 1: Confidence with a new map.

'In this hypnotic learning process...you have already learned many things of value and made some amazing changes...Many unconscious needs are being fulfilled, here...I'd like to thank your subconscious for everything it's done for you in your life...all the progress...the way it always protects and look out for you, the best way it knows how...Everyone is on their own journey...to do that well ***you need a good map***...If you get lost, you need a new map...to more accurately and safely navigate through this world...and when you update that map unconsciously...you ***fully believe that you can succeed, now...***

In order to succeed you need to ***feel confident about these changes...***In order to succeed you need to ***feel confident in their stability...***In order to succeed you need to ***feel 100% confidence in yourself, now...*** With these helpful ideas deeply embedded in your other mind...we can continue...because it's your unconscious beliefs that matter...When ***the unconscious beliefs are just there...***you can ***truly have supreme self-confidence in being free of x*** *(drug etc.)*

Step 2: Revivifying the 'no desire' state.

I know that ***you have more self-control than you know...***because I know there are times when you ***don't use x***...when ***you possess self-control...***It might be when you go on holiday/vacation... *(clients are always telling me how their problem/s disappear on holiday/vacation!)*

It might be a time when ***you simply cannot use x...***There may be times when you just naturally ***have no desire...***times when you are naturally happy...things are going well; times when you ***become absorbed by something very engaging...***So we know, and each and both of your know that there are times when ***you are in just the right frame of mind to demonstrate full self-control...now...***

You don't use it when you ***sleep soundly...*** There have been times when you may not have been 100% comfortable but there was ***no desire...***In this state of mind, now, you simply found ***no desire, no temptation at all...***As I talk about such times...and as you ***listen intently...***you can get in touch with this feeling of ***no desire...***Your subconscious knows its psychological and physiological component parts and will make it available to you more often, now...That state of mind and body can expand and amplify and intensify and strengthen as you turn a feeling into a colour that fills every part of you, with a state of ***no desire...***That's right! *(Key theme: feeling change through 'colour feelings'; see book 2.)* Let it expand till you feel it almost emanating from every part of you!

It's a pure, clean, healthy feeling and ***you enjoy no desire*** in that place...And what if and it can and you will do... *(mild confusion...)* ***No desire*** can lengthen and strengthen more and more and more...the time between can shrink to nothing...so all that is good is pleasantly uninterrupted...like when you ***ignore irrelevant signals, unconsciously.*** This is the easiest way to effortless be calm and so much more self-assured and relaxed, haven't you? Get to really own and ***possess that state of self-control*** and ***no desire...***Its power only grows...Its space inside and in time only grows...It lengthens, expands, fills, overwhelms and smothers...spreads into ***your much more positive future...***Goes beyond a passing phase...Goes beyond old perceived strategies for full-filling needs...Goes into the depths of your core and soul...beyond your waking name...All of this occurs in the safest, best and most appropriate way... *(safety feature.)*

If you need a cue word that you wish to say to yourself...to ***summon this state at will...*** Choose one because the subconscious is always listening and caring...Whenever you appropriately use it ***this new state is just there.*** And it's nice to know you ***have freewill and choice,*** didn't you? Won't you? And your self-confidence grows as this state of ***no desire is yours to keep...***each and both of you, now.

Step 3: Moving on, having no desire + reconnecting to your core values.

(No one really wants to be a junkie okay. Drugs

fundamentally violate the laws of being human – they degrade and abuse us, they violate our core sense of values as humans: honour, integrity, personal honesty, sincerity, compassion, ambition - a big one! - you name it, drugs dirty it! This module helps a person reconnect to core human values that can overpower addictive patterns of coping and move past the violation of those values – as symbolised by the drug/addiction 'relationship'.)

<u>Outgrowing an old real-hate-shun-ship.</u>

We have all reached times in our life when we knew it was right to...***move on from certain relationships...***It almost just happens...Our feelings alter...Our perceptions about that relationship alter as ***you mature, now...*** Some things that seemed so inviting at one stage in our life *('seem<u>ed</u>' = past tense)* just aren't, after a period of reflection, is that not so? Like a person you had a crush on... but then you realised it was just a type of puppy love and not the real thing at all. Because a really good relationship is mutually beneficial...based on caring, honesty, genuine support...There are key values that you have... you need to cherish them anew...

And you are ***feeling so much more relaxed*** as you ***listen with every cell in your body...*** as you have at important turning points of

fascination, now...There are times when you ***reach a turning point...***where you don't look back...when you just ***leave things that just don't fit anymore...***in the past...And no matter how old things might try to follow you... or snap at your heels...you know at times like those that...***you're 100% ready to stride out on your own, anew...***

Feelings can turn cold toward things that once excited, yesterday...no matter how it wriggles and tries to follow you...certain things can remain a memory of what was...You can ***take healthy desires with you*** into your future and find new, better expressions for their realisation in this reality, now...

We have all entered doors alone that were meaningful thresholds of expressing our true potential...and we only emerged enriched, did you not? Some things aren't fitted to fit through certain portals...No adjustments can shrink something that it too big...If ***you break free*** you just have to leave some things behind... dead weight as it were...Some things attract you more than any illusions of artificial satisfactions...Some things like...increased longevity...health...***a sense of self-respect, honour, honesty, integrity and decency, now...*** *(values are represented by nominalisations – throw in lots of platitudes!)* better relationships await you...And you

find these new ideas and approaches much more exciting, do you not? Will you not? ***Now...***

And when ***you commit 100% to healthy change*** you can take all your healthy pleasures with you into the future...Knowing, really knowing that genuine satisfaction is part of your new reality...

- What do you value most?
- What values had that past real-hate-shun-ship violated?
- How much has this process altered all that significantly? *(A beat only for each question.)*

A square peg can't fit through a round hole! There are things in this life that hold deeper meanings for you...And with this unconscious knowledge ***feel a great sense of relief sweep over you*** as you realise with every fibre of your being that ***you are over that*** and it feels GREAT!

And surprisingly, as you imagine stepping through a magical portal on my count of 1-2-3! You leave the truly unwanted behind you! All you need is within! Feel the release and clarity... Where are you not, that is much better to be? That's right! Sunshine is brighter! Scents more vividly alive! The whole world just seems a better place...Now...

Future pace: Dissociated rehearsal.

I'm simply going to be silent...And when I am for 30 seconds or so...in that ***healing*** time imagine, as though watching a movie of yourself...going through several times and places...that might arise where in your past you might have used x *(drug etc.)* But now...as if watching a movie...see yourself going through all those times...all those experiences...as a fully relaxed, calm, in control and confident x *(non-smoker/free you etc.)* now... *(Pause for 30 secs...)* That felt great didn't it? And you will, will you not? Will you not?

Associated experience.

And just for luck to embed these alterations of experience in your mind, now...Imagine ***going through those experiences with the better responses, feeling mastery over yourself*** and your life from the inside...Float into a time and go through the better way of being...responding...feeling...living... experiencing...reconnecting to your core human values...Do that as many times as your unconscious knows...that you need to ***own these changes unconsciously, now...***And the duration of a pause is more than enough in trance...Perfect. *(Wait 30 seconds again...)*

Good – you have done magnificently! How things happened is not as relevant as that they had. Wasn't it? You only ***feel total freedom, now.*** That's right.'

Metaphor 2: Disconnection symbology module.

(A useful symbology metaphor which has already been touched upon is anything that represents letting go of, dissociating from, leaving in the past, detaching from any old addictive behaviour/substance etc. The following can be used with multiple addictions as and when needed.)

The poisoned vat/tank symbology.

'Up until now you have been doing x *(drug etc.)* In order to ***fully disconnect from that, now...***I want you to visualise a huge vat/tank of all the toxins and poisons that you had been allowing into your system...And it is connected to your body by some kind of awful looking pipe or tube...

Look at that vat/tank of all that disgusting junk that you *had* been damaging that wonderful mind and body with...Were you born for that? No; so as you look at that vile vat/tank of poisons...recognise at a very deep level that...

you are worth far more than that. Looking at all that swilling discoloured filth allows you to...***develop a broader, more realistic perspective on things...***You know, really know that the time for change is now...

And the great thing is all you have to do to... ***unconsciously let go of all those old patterns...***is to disconnect that pipe safely and easily and push that vat/tank of garbage as far away as it will go in your mind...Not now but soon, when I say 'Now!' you can do that. Get ready with an inner resolve and determination to ***sever that abusive relationship with x (drug/addiction etc.) once and for all...***

Okay! Are you ready to get that disgusting monkey off your back! 'Now!' That's it. Remove it and push it far away – you have all the strength you need in trance...As soon as you have done that... *(Pause just a beat!)* You start to ***feel free and independent*** of that rubbish...You instantly ***feel better*** in yourself... Your mind and body ***feel purified*** and clean... You ***feel well*** and in control again. And that is a pretty good feeling to feel, isn't it?

You can take this act as a sign and a signal that anyone can...***leave the unwanted in the past, now...***And a real truism about all human beings is they...***adapt very quickly to changes, now.*** Well done! You are doing very well etc.'

(Slot this in where and when you feel it's best.)

<u>Metaphor 3: Cleaning up the mess.</u>

(Drugs have connotations of being 'dirty', of causing damage to the body etc. And rightly so. A hypnotic 'clean-up operation' can suggest that the body is starting to cleanse itself, to detox as it were. If appropriate, try the following...)

<u>The clean place inside.</u>

'Imagine now that you are walking down a path through a beautiful natural place...somewhere special that appeals to you...Might be a meadow...a mountain...could be through a large forest...That's it. Just get the sense of being there...so relaxed...so calm...Notice the environment...take in all the details...make it vivid and real...as if you're there not here... Might be vegetation, flowers...smells and sounds that make the whole experience lifelike...Be aware of these inner sensory qualities...This place only adds to your feeling of comfort...

And now...you can see a building that represents your body...the health and integrity of that body...that survival mechanism that you were born with...that you are meant to take care of...See your body symbolised by some kind of building not far ahead...Might be on a hill...Might be in a valley...Could be a palace... Could be a cottage...Trust whatever the subconscious offers you to symbolise that...

Once you can see that clearly and are happy with it at all levels...I want you to walk up to and enter that place...If it has doors notice they open easily...I'll be quiet for 10 seconds while you do that... *(Do so...)*

As you ***go inside*** notice how dirty, unkempt and dingy it has become...you don't like the look of it one bit...it needs a spring clean...The owner...the occupier hasn't looked after it as they should...you instinctively sense this...The air might be fetid (foul), thick and dusty? I don't know...You wonder how anyone could ***live comfortably*** in such a place...Deep inside you realise it's time to ***clean that place up...***Deep inside you recognise its time that ***you take care of that place*** in the right way.

Find the kitchen sink in that place...you'll find cleaning equipment there...brooms nearby... whatever you need to ***clean up that place unconsciously*** is there...*(Quiet for a beat or two to allow them to 'locate it'.)* I will be quiet for a whole minute soon...and you have all the time you need to do what you know needs to be done to help you ***satisfy your real needs...***Clean that place up in the pause/pores...and watch as the whole place becomes progressively cleaner...watch as it is purified...Notice how just under the muck, dirt and grime ***there is a natural beauty inside...***that you are revealing and appreciating...perhaps for the first time in a long time...You ***feel a desire to keep this place clean, now...***Go ahead and complete that cleaning process. *(Quiet for 1 whole minute!)*

Excellent! Give yourself a pat on the back as it were! Look how clean and pure that place is... this special place...a place made to help you get your needs met for...security...comfort...natural pleasure...shelter...protection...and so much more...and ponder, now, all your body does for you...Ponder its strength and attractiveness... perhaps consider some aspect of what it does that you had given little thought to before...And at a deep level of information processing know you MUST...***treat that body with love and respect from now on.*** That's right!

That's what mature, responsible people do, do they not? And ***you are such a person, now...*** Feel the joy and already returning vitality you feel there, deep inside...The air seems purified as it is on a nature walk...The colours brighter, more vivid and alive...In fact you ***feel***

enlivened as a result of this process. All the pleasures of the senses are naturally heightened...smells smell richer...sounds are clearer and more vibrant...tastes are returning, changing and enhanced...All these changes make ***you feel more alive!*** All these changes make ***you love and appreciate this life!*** All these changes make you ***determined and focused!*** All these changes ensure that ***you stay on track, forever!*** You can take this act as a sign and a signal that...***you have succeeded, now...***in all the right ways that meet your unique needs. When you ***stay relaxed*** your creativity helps...Thaaaa-aaat's right!'

Case 8: Healing heroin interventions.

Heroin is a nasty, horrid drug. It is little known that many opium addicts were unwittingly created by doctors during World War 2 whilst treating pain caused by combat wounds. My grandfather included. Serious users will almost always need medical help to come off of heroin – using methadone etc.. Why? Because heroin withdrawal can be very dangerous. However hypnosis can help addicts who have used heroin. If a person has only used heroin once, and that does happen, it is not always instantly addictive (as many believe); the user, dumb as they are, may well never use it again. Obviously the best thing is to not even try it! But the people coming to see you will be beyond that point. Way beyond it!

Often heroin use is linked to trauma, depression, very low self-worth etc. and you will have to do work on those areas too. It is often a bit like severe alcoholism – it is an obliteration tactic of painful reality drug. This often entails child abuse – not always, and not necessarily sexual, it can just be an overly critical, unloving, perfectionist parent/s who can be the prime cause. Sometimes the person just hangs around with 'the wrong people' and before they know it, they've been dragged down into heroin hell by such losers. Some people do use drugs as a lifestyle choice: they fantasise that's that how humans are supposed to live. If you are a normal hypnotherapist with a nice suburban practise you may come across no heroin clients in years, if ever! However, knowing what to do can only help your overall skills.

If you are working with a client who is undergoing medical intervention/s for such a problem, ensure that what you do compliments the work of doctors and nurses etc. This does not mean you take orders from such people. *Your professional relationship is with your client.* It is they and they alone who have the last word on receiving help from you. Nothing in the script that follows will interfere with anything other healthcare professionals are doing. There is however no one more qualified to help a suffering person with the mental and emotional aspects of drug use and withdrawal than a good hypnotherapist. And that's you buster! Experience helps too.

The tricks you learn in this procedure can be applied to other addictions where necessary, using your own judgement and making needed alterations etc. Moreover - I suggest that you rewrite all scripts in this book - improve them, make them your own, add other things you already do that work; most importantly make the language your own – if you simplify stuff in real life, do that to the scripts. ***Techniques only really work when you personalise***

them. I have no idea why no other hypnotist has not EVER put all these addiction busting techniques together in one place as a resource for fellow professionals of all varieties and trainings and the wider public who are fascinated by hypnosis???! I had to write this book because no one else has, that I know! What you are learning here could take a beginner *years* to accumulate in terms of techniques, courses and experience – that's not good enough. I have saved you more heartache and cash in this book than you know!!! That was one of my major motivations in creating this book series.

Interestingly heroin users can quit spontaneously without medical help: once Vietnam veterans left the utter insanity of a war zone which had provoked them into heroin use by preventing them from getting pretty much ANY of their genuine universal human needs met and returned home, many no longer felt such a sense of a total loss of normality and simply stopped using the drug. Loving homes, being around people who care about you deeply and the myriad pleasures of everyday life alone can be very healing indeed. ***No drug is more powerful than the power of the human spirit, human love, and human healing potentials accessible in SANE environments.***

As a therapist you should know that the fact that the vulnerable client knows you competently care about their welfare is more beneficial than any statistician can measure. Addicts need to know you do care. You should subcommunicate this in everything you do – starting with the initial phone call etc.

As with all addiction use parts negotiation script 2 before doing the following BUT make sure you throw in some suggestions to the effect that the person will only stop using heroin at the right rate and speed etc. – see the section on treating alcoholism.

The hope beyond heroin script.

(Again parts work is needed too. Deep hypnosis assumed...)

Step 1: The land of the Lotus eater's metaphor.

'There is a place ***beyond the reach of heroin, now...***And that reminds me of the story of Odysseus...You may have heard the tale...***as a child, now...***about 'The land of the Lotus-Eaters'...On sailing back home from Troy... a rogue north wind had blown the sea captain and his crew off course...they had arrived at a mysterious island...to which they never intended to visit...The people who lived there were called 'Lotophagi'... *(pronounced: Loto-far-jee)* the

Lotus-Eaters...They did nothing but eat lotuses...Odysseus sent his scouts to venture inland...After several days and having heard nothing from the scouts...Odysseus set out with a small group of his men...soon they found the scouts eating the mysterious lotus...with the Lotus-Eaters...

The scouts did not want to leave...The Lotus-Eaters entreated Odysseus and his men to join them...The scouts told their captain how lotuses make you ***fall into a blissful oblivion...***A place where ***you become unmindful...***where you can ***forget about your cares*** for a while...

But Odysseus was the captain and knew what was really best for his crew...The men were dragged back against their protests and chained to the oars...The reason the captain did this is because he knew, at a fundamental level...we need the challenges of life...we need to have problems that we overcome...we cannot hide from the process of living...When you ***engage fully with the ups and downs of life...***you mature beyond the illusions of the no life lotus eaters. Ask yourself this: is your time that un-precious? With this reality in mind we can continue...

Step 2: Heroin as a poisoning psychopath metaphor.

(Here, again, we are comparing drugs to an abusive relationship.)

Have you ever heard those tales of women who married certain men? Men that their friends could see through...but that they couldn't... Those types of men are good with words...they know what to say to seduce any woman...they have a certain superficial charm...

At first everything seems to be fine...until the lady finds herself isolated from her friends...And before she knows it, that type of man has slowly eroded her confidence and self-respect... He has simply stopped telling her what he wanted her to hear...

We are so adaptable that we may believe that the abnormal is normal...Now there is only the unmasked bully or worse...Now there is only pain where there was once a type of joy...Now there is only degradation...Now there is only despair...And for some, for those fooled by the sweet words of the psychopath there may be a grimmer fate still...That of a slow kind of duel poisoning of the mind and body...gradually eroding all of your self-worth...

And if another kind of toxicity continues, the

woman may be killed...What it takes is only the strength of a person to ***see what is....***When we ***recognise certain realities*** we can ***make the decision deep inside to break free, change and move on, now...***There is after all only so much abuse that anyone can take. With that in mind and as another part of you considers realities, consequences and prospects...in many different ways, as I talk of other things, we can continue...

The worst of the bad things have not happened...nothing like that is inevitable... the only inevitability is ***change...***

Step 3: Switching off addictive voices.

(Key hypnotic theme: 'ignoring certain messages' - drugs/addictions create messages in the brain; these can be ignored, as in the case of pain. Depression does a similar thing.)

Some messages we need to listen to...they help us...they lead us where we need to go...on our journey in life...Some voices hypnotise us with good advice...Some lie to us with a negative kind of hypnosis...They tell us that fantasy is real...that the impossible is possible...but the good thing is you have powerful unconscious mechanisms that protect you from obvious lies...You have a powerful conscious mind that can ***criticise and evaluate information,***

inside and out accurately...

Have you ever noticed how when some people talk ***you pay attention to this person*** (?) And with others ***you ignore unhealthy messages*** with a firm conviction of what is truly right and wrong for you...What if you could imagine turning down the volume of a particular lying voice or voices so that ***you can't hear it anymore*** or it sounds weak, feeble and distant, far off, inaudible, indistinct, mumbly...Or like a voice you instinctively disbelieve.

If it helps, imagine a control panel that allows this adjustment. But your unconscious can ***do this*** for you ***unconsciously, now...*** *(Hypnotic coding.)* That's it...Good.

Step 4: Kick-starting the recovery process.

The process is well underway when ***you deeply want recovery...***Have you ever gone for something with all your heart and soul? The good thing about your mind and body is that... ***you know how to heal unconsciously...***All you have to do is ***decide to STOP, NOW!*** And when you do...certain processes come into play that ease your recovery, assist your purpose without you even knowing how. And that's nice to know isn't it? For there is what you might call...a healing part of you...The healing ability of humans is amazing...because we all ***have a***

natural inclination toward good health...

Now, this part gets rid of discomfort over time... it can ***heal old wounds...***it can ***restore good feelings and thoughts...***And there is also a far deeper part of you that is much stronger than you imagine...Patterns are just that...like fish that swim across the surface of a pond...like the changing seasons...like passing moods...like sand in the hand on windy days...like the comings and goings of people, places, *(NFH: this says to the subconscious – 'What I want you to do is like this.' See 'Forbidden hypnotic secrets')* things and ways of being and doing... Yet far beneath the surface there is more than that which passes temporally in and then out of anyone's experiences...

I know there have been many times when ***you outgrow things that are outdated, now.*** You can get that knowing feeling...that lets you know...***you will recover fully, now.*** Because I know that each and both of you know how to ***regain full health.***

Step 5: Dealing with addiction's positive intent.

I would like to thank that part of you that compelled you back then...to do what you don't anymore, wasn't it? It had its good reasons but when you ***find more important reasons to change, unconsciously...***why stick with old technologies that are past their prime when... you can ***own better ways of doing things...*** *(?)*

And your powerful creative part can and will help, now. It is working effortlessly when you ***relax about so many things...***You see, ***your calming mind, now...***functions at its best when you trust other than conscious processes...to do what they do...If you have an outcome, it's always best to ***find the best solution...***to ***generate many solutions*** and find the finest in experience, is that not so? You reach any destination by knowing exactly where you are going...For that you need a good map... Certain former, inappropriate processes... responses...sensations...perceptions...that upheld that unwanted habit...can somehow be inhibited, now. That's right.

You are not a 'heroin addict' ***you are a free person...*** *(Or use whatever words they use to describe health – key theme: 'feed-back their own words' to them; they are neurological keys!)* You are not an ex addict ***you are a free person...***Free people do not obsess or crave that which can never truly satisfy. And there's a truth in that. Free people have ***no unhealthy urges or cravings...***If a part is sending a message and the situation changes...inside and out, isn't it best to ***send better messages...*** (?)

And as you are so much more soothed and calmed inside...***this new identity becomes your 100% total reality, now.*** You can't continue being who you weren't. Is that not so?

Step 6: Colour feelings of personal power.

Imagine a colour that represents your personnel feelings of power...they are linked to your inner strength! That's the way...Let that colour expand from where it is...And as it does so...let it grow brighter and stronger, amplified and more intense...And as the colour changes and expands ***beyond old perceived limits...***you ***feel your personal power grow*** and grow... More and more and more! *(A beat...)* Double it! *(A beat...)* And double it again! *(A beat...)* Thaaa-aat's it!

This hypnotically healing process is ***reconnecting you to your power!*** Your power to choose! Your power to overcome! Your power to surpass! Your power to endure and emerge afresh, as a new dawn! That's right! ***Feeling that sense of power flood all through your mind-body system powerfully, now!*** Feel it emanate out beyond you so anyone at all would ***notice the difference!*** This feeling radiates beyond you! Almost as if you are glowing with it! To recall this feeling at will, unconsciously, say a trigger word to yourself – something like 'POWER'!

And ***this feeling will be there*** when you need it, now. *(Triggers can ease a client's conscious mind that the resource is 'callable' on cue.)* This is a post...hypnotic...command!

There are so many more wonderful emotions to choose from...Fantastic! You are doing really well! Thoughts, feelings, choices, adjustments, attitudes, patterns and point of view can and do ***change effectively*** just when you need it. The benefits are priceless. There is a saying... *'He/she who has health has hope and she/he who has hope has everything.'* Keep your sense of your personal power turbo-boosted as a deserved gift for yourself!

As a result of these changes past impressions of what you used to label *(the word 'impressions' is suggestive of weakness)* ***'temptation' seems far less tempting*** somehow. And that's nice to know, haven't you?

Step 6: Playing with the sense of healing time.

(Key theme – time distortion!)

They say timing is everything...and your sense of time is controlled by your unconscious mind... It can slow or speed your perception of time up or down... *(Mild confusion.)* It can ensure that ***difficult times seem to pass quickly...*** It can ensure that ***your healing seems to happen***

quickly...It can slow down the good times so you fully relish the experience...Any temporary passing feelings during withdrawal that are less than 100% comfortable...can pass so quickly... before you know it they're gone...and you can ***feel clean, pure and strong inside...***

Suggestive emotional future pace to a healed time.

(Future pacing doesn't have to always be about imagining change – you can feel change too.)

There is rain before the sunshine...the end of winter already shows signs of spring. It can be motivating to ***feel a foretaste of the good times...***times beyond healing when ***you are healed...***What if you could ***feel healed now...*** (?) What if you could ***feel totally free of drugs for good...*** (?) What if you could ***feel deep joy...*** (?) What if you could ***feel satisfaction...*** (?) The process of healing had occurred and ***you simply feel healthy,*** again...You see, I know you have felt these things before...and what you did once you can do again only better...Your mind-body knows the psychological and physiological component parts of ***you're feeling healed, does it not?*** And you can trust that ***the subconscious will provide such feelings*** and more in the days and weeks of success that lie ahead, now. As though ***all your motivation and the energy***

of your life force is coming back to you... That's right.

Handling physical withdrawal sub module.

As if then could become now, wasn't it? As if your deeper mind knows how to ignore or go around...somehow...certain signals... ***discomfort can be lessened to manageable levels...***That's it. Signals can alter in intensity...diminish in amplitude...or at least be lessened considerably...As there are parts of you that communicate discomfort but in certain circumstances they do alter their communications outputs to consciousness...a stab can become a warmth...many more ways than one to communicate an intent...A deeper part of you is aware of them so you don't have to be so much as ***that body detoxifies*** in the healthiest, safest, best way possible and only at the right rate and speed...your unconscious knows what is best...trust that it will guide you expertly in this process...

Time consciousness, certain feelings and more will change as need be so that...***the healing process is easier than you had imagined...*** It's nice to know that consciously and unconsciously, ***you have far more control than you realised...***Good!

Step 7: Weaning metaphor.

(Key theme: 'maturation'.)

Children need the joy of mother's breast until a certain age...We all know children who suck their thumb...At the right age having a good old thumb suck is just fine and dandy...but all it does is allow a person to ***access inherent feelings of comfort, inside, now.*** I know a little girl who loves her Nu-Nu – that's her blankie! When she was a baby she loved to hold it and stroke her forefinger through it! It can allow you to ***experience feelings of profound well-being.*** She'd hum with comfort. And if that Nu Nu got lost she would not ***be happy*** and we'd have to hunt around till we found that Nu-Nu! If we didn't, there would be big trouble!

And I saw a young man who couldn't stop sucking his thumb before bed...and he was nearly 20! But the things is – sooner or later we realise that ***re-accessing your comfort...***lies not outside, in things, but inside, in you...At some point we ***mature*** and somehow we.. ***develop the flexibility...***to wean ourselves off of the unnecessary, now. Because that's just a part of being you.

Step 8: Profound relaxation through the reality of caring.

(Key theme: a relaxed mind and body is creative and healthy.)

Did you know that just being shown pictures of others being loved and cared for can ***reduce the brain's response to threat*** (?) In fact when you ***see pictures of humans loving and caring…***and even if old images of grimaces and grumpy folk are shown too… ***your amygdala does not respond to perceived threats as it once did.*** It's as if, even in formerly anxious people…just being reminded you are loved and cared for…helps ***really dampen certain responses considerably…***As it's nice to know you can ***feel supported in your efforts somehow…***

Step 9: Utilising forgetting.

(Key theme: 'amnesia'.)

When we are learning something we need to ***pay close attention…***but we also need to ***ignore irrelevant things*** once we had learned them…In a way we are always forgetting things and paying attention to more important things as we progress through life…There were certain habits you had…certain people you knew…and at the time they *seemed* important…And then without knowing how or why you ***just forget to recall it.*** *(This utilises 'rolling consciousness' – see 'Wizards of trance'.)* Other things dominated the forefront and background of your thinking...you learned, really learned to ***process information differently.*** Things can amplify or recede... seem big then appear small...things diminish... fade and eventually, slip away into old forgotten things of yester year, now.

Sometimes the tighter you ***TRY in vain*** to hold something...the harder it is to hold on. That's a paradoxical paradox!

Step 10: Re-setting linguistic associations.

(Drug lingo and jargon can be destabilised in hypnosis...)

Brown is the colour of faeces/shit. *(I would just say 'shit' personally!)* Opium is no-hope-scum. Heroine is no hero in this life. Certain meanings to ***old symbolic triggers can be negatively associated to*** from now on...And the power of your own creative language capacity will be of spontaneous assistance when needed. You can ***re-link to old and associate to new, pleasurable, healthy sets of associations instantly...***Some things are scrambled and unscrambled all in one go! The *emotional* meaning, flavour of words can ***shift***

appropriately...in ways that surprise and delight you, now.

<u>*Step 11: Utilising already existing natural joys – the sea of bliss!*</u>

(Key theme: 'revivifying natural pleasure'.)

Imagine something neutral like a blank sheet of paper...***Relax 10 times deeper*** in your own way...Imagine you are floating on what I call 'The Sea of Bliss'. You ***feel safe and completely secure*** inside as you just float...As you ride the current, safely, there, on the waves of your inner delight...so ***gentle, peaceful and free...***you can grow to understand that... by simply ***drifting*** in this place...you ***start to reconnect to your ample good feelings...*** It's as if you ***become absorbed by natural good feelings*** in this place...Notice how much better you feel already...

Now, as you float, and as I am quiet as a mouse...your wondrous unconscious self will create an experience in the silence...I don't know what it will be or should be...your deeper mind is FAR wiser...and in this experience you will **feel a series of quite amazing feelings...**feelings that will convince you that... you have all the uppers and downers you need inside of you, naturally...Feelings that make you ***bathe in pleasure of a simply***

indescribable kind. I will be quiet for a full minute...and in that time and on my cue...and in deep hypnotic trance now...you will ***feel a building bliss beyond words...***And the cue word is simply 'BLISS!' *(Wait a beat...)* 'Bliss!' That's it.

(Shhh for 1 minute; look out for signs of bliss...)

You can take this act as a sign and a signal that...***all the pleasure you need is within you...***so that you feel, really ***feel high on life...***knowing that you have a wide range of emotional responses and they all tell you something that can help you and move your life forward when you...***pay attention to what they are telling you, now...***

Step 12: Getting needs met naturally.

(Key theme: need satisfaction = real satisfaction.)

One of the reasons you were stuck back then was because you had failed to get certain needs met...Needs that are essential to ***you're feeling good naturally...***Could be an emotional need - say the need for positive attention. Could be a physical need – say the need for good food and exercise. Could be a need related to relationships – say your need to ***feel loved unconditionally, now...***That being so, you can let a deeply personal need come to mind...That's it. One that you know needs satisfying to ensure your success. So right now...

Imagining getting a need met sub-module.

(Dissociated practise.)

With that in mind...just focus on the need to meet that need...conjure up some scene in your mind – watching it from the outside...a time from ***your brighter future...***when this need is being met in a genuinely pleasant and satisfying way...because you are taking action in reality to make it so.

Your creative part will help you solve any problems that arise...Just get the sense of that time...like having a pleasant daydream...Notice - What you're doing...How that you is feeling... Notice the different responses you are getting... Relax as you learn from that...I'll be quiet for 15 seconds or so while you practise that. *(Do so.)* Good!

Associated practise.

Now using the powerful inner focus of this state...knowing that this relaxation allows your access to new creative ideas and associations which manifest in delightful and surprising ways...better ones that move you forward... When you are ready...glide with poise into that scene...with you getting that need for x *(security/work etc.)* met...See through those eyes...Hears through those ears...***Feel how much more confident and light-hearted you feel*** while getting that need met pleasantly...

You can do it because you're human and humans, like plants, ***instinctively know how to do certain things...***That better future-present, now...Again I'll be quiet for a full 20 seconds while you go through that...to each and both of your satisfaction. *(Do so.)* In fact – ***feel a foretaste of that satisfaction now...***That's right! You are learning at deep levels... Experientially is the best way. That's right. Good. *(NFH: you can go through 3-5 need rehearsals if you wish or just say... 'At a deep level of mentation, perhaps while you sleep and dream at night your curious unconscious mind will rehearse ways that will ensure you **get your genuine needs satisfied, now.'** Or just say, 'The mind can generalise from a learning, can it not?')*

Step 13: Removing feelings of temptation symbology.

(Key theme: 'symbology manipulation' adjusts feelings and so thoughts. Thoughts emerge

from feelings not the other way around.)

Now we are going to do something that will ***smother any old feelings of temptation for drug x (heroin etc.), unconsciously.***

Getting rid of unwanted feelings script.

(This is adapted from a script in book 6, 'Crafting hypnotic spells'. Deep hypnosis assumed...)

Phase 1: Remove feelings of temptation state.

(The urge to take any drug is a feeling: in hypnosis we can powerfully alter ANY feeling!)

Ok so you want to get rid of that old urge to use x *(heroin etc.)* that feeling/emotion etc... Ok...just simply imagine that old unwanted feeling, that state...as an object or symbol of some kind...Trust whatever the subconscious offers without question...it knows exactly what it's doing...Notice it's qualities...it's size...Notice the colour or colours of it...If you could handle it how much would it weigh approximately? Does it have a particular shape at all? How solid is it? Can you see through it? What kind of texture has it got, if you were able to feel it? Notice any temperature or variations of warmth...Is it cold? Dry or moist? Really get to know it intimately.

(Allow some processing time 7-10 seconds or so.)

Great! Take this symbolic object or whatever it is...and put it into some holding device from which escape is impossible...Seal that device so that you are 100% certain that it is solidly closed...If you want you can chain it, solder it, super glue it shut...Do anything you need to do in your imagination...to ensure ***it is forever locked within that container***... *(You can hypnotically store emotions in symbolic 'containers'. 'Mazing!)*

Once that's done, you can do the following... Push it far away from you...shove it to the other side of the space you're in...push it off a high cliff so that it shatters below...or floats off to sea...blow it up with a cartoon bomb...shoot it out into the depths of space attached to a man-less rocket...perhaps it gets swallowed by a black hole... (?) Symbolically do whatever you associate with your natural ability to ***GET RID OF THAT FEELING, unconsciously, now...***

Great...You'll find, if you were to attempt to locate that ***old state...***that it's ***gone completely*** or very ***much more diminished...*** *(This is 'hypnotic coding' again. The broken code embed is – 'Old state gone completely, much more diminished.' Hedge your bets!)* certainly changed for the better...

Step 2: Lock in a good symbolic state!

So now we've done that...what object/symbol/colour would fully represent... ***you're feeling great and totally free be*** (?) You want a state that represents the opposite of the old, unwanted one. So that ***you aren't bothered by anything like that, anymore...Now,*** no worries or troubles... anymore...***no problem whatsoever...***So that...***you're feeling extremely good and so confident!*** *(Allow up to 10 seconds for this to happen – you will develop a 'feeling' over time when they have done this.)*

Ok...Go through the process you did before...be aware of shape, size, weight, solidity or otherwise, relative warmth and textures etc.... any and all relevant things so that you really get to know this new resourceful feeling or set of them...I'll be quiet as you do... *(Pause 10 seconds etc.)* Brilliant!

Now we know that all feelings feel right somewhere in our bodies...it's the only way they make sense...so take this symbol/feeling and place it inside you where it feels...absolutely right and perfect...That's it, find that place... just the right place for you today... *(Allow a further 10 seconds for placement.)*

Allow that wonderful feeling to spread out

– all through your mind and body...***lock it in solidly and keep it...Now,*** let it fully and gloriously radiate from you...throughout your mind and body...in an advantageously wonderful way...***letting that feeling expand and grow bigger...***and bigger and even more intense so that it fills you with ***sensational feelings from head to toe*** right now and in your better feeling future! Fan-tastic!

You have done really well. Now you have done this know – you can ***choose how you feel...*** you ***have more control over your emotions*** and so much more. Good!

Step 14: Summation future pace – dissociated.

Imagine now on a movie screen, and knowing that ***you are the director of this process...*** see that you going through that healing process of detoxification as pleasantly as you are reasonably able...You might notice that you really does ***feel far less excitable*** and dis-***comfort more...less rawness, irritation and sensitivity...***That you can ***focus fully*** on their worthy goal...You can see them laughing, joking even, smiling...so ***your health returns fully*** faster than you thought. And in some amazing way you just know ***you have what it takes to succeed...Will power strong! Determination enhanced...***You are calmer and even happier than you'd imagined and as a consequence that part that had worried and that looks out for danger can ***feel reassured you'll be fine.*** Sometimes we have to feel a bit of discomfort before we get to the really good times...That's just life.

There's a saying – 'When the going gets tough the tough get going!!!' And ***you are far tougher than you know!*** Your ancestors survived many things...giant animals, geological catastrophes, wars and much worse...this healing process is but a tiny time in your life... You can see that person can handle that which arises before it passes...And sooner than you know it...that you can - ***feel so strong inside!*** That you can – ***feel cleansed and purified!*** The body knows what to do! Before you know it that essential healing process is over and you ***feel 100% healthy once more...***

All suffering passes...and what you learned can make it all worthwhile somehow...***forgive yourself your mistakes...***Focus on your much better future! You may even look back and laugh! Natural pleasures now attract you... tastes, simple things...sights...people... companionship...the light at certain times of day...atmospheres...colours and sounds make you ***feel a natural buzz*** about living...the anticipation of a real reward, now.

See that you going through a whole day

clean and healthy and free! while I'm quiet... *(Not a word for a full minute...I dissociate them from the process so the coming unpleasantness is lessened. They aren't fully immersed in it!)*

Future pace associated.

Imagine now a future you who has already gone through that process. See them healthy and happy and enjoying their life...When ***you're ready...***float into that future present you! See through those eyes – you did it! You ***believe in your capacity to do so*** with every fibre of your being! Hear through those ears – ***feel that powerful sense of control*** returned and locked in tight! ***Feel how good you feel to be clean and clear*** – fresh and so healthy in mind and body! Wow! That really is something! And all these learnings and healings...states of mind and body will simply be automatically available to you without any external aids or tricks...just when you need it, and this is so. All you need do is say your special word – 'POWER!' or whatever else you prefer...and ***these powerful resources you have reconnected to will arise!***

And if any silly ideas of going back were to flit through your mind...without knowing how, you can ***simply dissociate from those old desires completely now.*** You and they are not connected, ***no old desires*** any...more...

You might even observe them in passive amusement...like driftwood on the sea. and that's that.

Step 15: Direct suggestions + finalisation process.

Starting and completing right now...lifestyle changes occur...changes in perceptions manifest...patterns alter...habits of many kinds are modified...feelings and states are appropriately enhanced and diminished... thinking, beliefs and behaviours can and do ***change beneficially...***And whatever else the subconscious mind knows needs to occur now, only in the safest ways at all times, come to pass as this person's 100% total, personal drug free reality!

Going back to the past seems silly, ludicrous – it can't happen! ***You are a free and healthy person...***Reconnections, re-associations of already existing subconscious structures materialise, powerfully now! You fully welcome and comprehend that ***these changes have been made.*** That's right!'

Analysis:

With heroin addiction we are building in abilities that should make it easier for a person to come off of the drugs as easily as is possible. Unlike the other sessions, severe alcoholism aside, we might not see 'instant results', in that the individual may have a medical treatment program that must be adhered to. The above should however make that process a whole lot easier and much less painful. A good thing. It is longer than the others as we have to re-access far more resources in order to ensure success. We are dipping into the unconscious and saying, 'You'll need a bit of that and this, oh and don't forget two of them etc.!'

End note: Grab heroin addiction by the balls and bombard it into submission. Leave that disgusting life rot no way back: be comprehensive, take your time and triumph!

Myths of the 'craving brain'.

Misery/stress does not make people seek to 'bio-balance' the brain. Whatever that crap means. A book, 'The Craving Brain: A Bold New Approach to Breaking Free from Drug Addiction, Overeating, Alcoholism, Gambling' by doctors Ronald A. Ruden and Marcia Byalick claims otherwise. 'The Craving brain' spread this idea amongst certain unthinking circles. So-called 'uncontrollable urges' are such because the subconscious has taken over control of them. The book advocates meditation to help: meditation is so dangerous it can drive you insane!!! See book 7 in my series, 'Escaping cultural hypnosis'.

The authors are right about one thing – the destruction of a dominant culture leads to mass drug addiction. This is what we are experiencing in the West: its decline! If you note the following guidelines below and in the next section, those 'uncontrollable urges' (you never ONCE controlled them? Ever?!) vanish: go figure!!! As a therapist you need specific tricks to get someone out of the hole they have dug themselves into.

NOTE 1: we do know from studies that tiredness and stress make people more prone to indulge in any kind of 'tempting' act. This being so hypnosis is ideally

suited to restoring a sense of calm and energy: it also allows us to speak to the 'emotional part' of the brain and alter any emotions intensity or context that is being expressed.

Note 2: If someone is calm and happy and getting their needs met they can beat addiction without any therapy.

The missing needs of people experiencing addiction processes.

For a full list of the key questions and theory behind my theory on the importance of addressing clients missing needs to solve any presenting problem/problem matrix see 'Powerful hypnosis' and the appendix of 'Wizards of trance'. When you speak to hypnotherapy clients, it don't take long folks to work out that *something is missing* in this person's life. Such as:

- They don't have a boyfriend/girlfriend/partner/wife husband.
- They have family problems.
- They have no one or few people who really appreciate them unconditionally.
- Their life or lack of one lacks meaning and purpose.
- They aren't achieving deeply desired goals.
- They lack a sense of security: at home, work etc.
- They don't have enough small daily pleasures etc.

- They want children and don't have them.
- They have an unsupportive spouse etc.
- They were overly criticised as children.
- They lacked unconditional love as children.
- They have a really crap social life.
- They focus on themselves too much.
- They have no connection to something 'bigger' than themselves – God, country, heck even a sport will do!
- They lack any sense of community or involvement in it.
- They feel isolated.

You could go on: just ask – ***what's missing?*** Sometimes I just say, 'Something's missing in your life; what is it? What is not in your life that you need to feel good naturally?' ***We have been so dehumanised and live is such fake, artificial societies that people have lost touch with what it truly means to be human.*** Sad isn't it? A list of specific questions follows to show I am not a cheap bastard who is trying to con you into buying my other books – do go read 'em though.

Universal human needs quiz.

I usually save this for a 2nd session. I see if a client sorts themselves out. If they come back to see me again, I nearly always systematically check for missing needs: you can cover this in hypnosis through imaginative rehearsal of getting those needs met BUT I usually (99% of the time) just point out the facts to a client and tell 'em they have to get specific needs met to feel well – they always do their homework!

These questions ascertain the degree to which universal human needs are being met NOW. You do not have to ask all of them; I usually ask 12 or so that seem relevant: hopefully they'll stimulate you to formulate your own. The list is taken from the appendix in my 5th book 'Wizards of trance' and reprinted here for ease of reference and because I am a generous, cuddly teddy bear by nature.

AGAIN! Underlying presupposition – what is missing in this person's life?

1. Are you eating healthily?
2. Are you exercising regularly?
3. Do you feel isolated and if so is that a problem?
4. Do you have enough friends?
5. Do you have a good social life?
6. Do you receive enough positive attention

from others?

7. Do you feel psychologically secure?
8. Are you financially secure?
9. Are you secure at home/in your closest relationships?
10. Is your work/job fulfilling?
11. Is your work/life balance as you wish it to be?
12. Do you spend enough time with your family?
13. Do you feel you have enough time?
14. Do you feel you give enough good quality attention to others?
15. Do you feel you help other people enough?
16. Do you feel you have enough space or too little space around you? Is the lack stressful?
17. Are you overly bored?
18. Are you overstressed/overloaded?
19. Are you loved, appreciated for the totality of who you are, in all ways, unconditionally or otherwise by at least one person?
20. Do you feel connected to something 'bigger' than yourself? Group? Cause? Religion? Politics etc.?
21. Do you feel you have sufficient control/influence in your life?
22. Are you honestly able to get privacy when needed?
23. Do you have at least one genuinely close friend?
24. Do you feel an emotional connection in your life to enough people in ways that satisfy you?

25. Is your social status/role/s important to you? And if so, is it appreciated and acknowledged? (This can be son, daughter, wife, dad etc. as well as a work role.)
26. Do you feel valued as a family member?
27. Do you feel valued at work?
28. Do you feel able/talented/competent in at least one if not more areas of life?
29. Are you mentally and physically stretched in ways you find meaningful?
30. Do you treat yourself often enough?
31. Do you get enough fresh air and sunshine?
32. Do you get out into the country often enough?
33. Is there something missing from your life?
34. Do you experience sufficient natural pleasures in daily, day to day living?
35. Is your sense of curiosity about the world around you satisfied?
36. Is your sex life satisfying? (May not be best to ask during therapy. Note it for yourself as you talk to a client. Are they getting enough?)
37. Do you feel enough other people find you attractive?
38. What would you do with your life if you knew you could only succeed?
39. What are you most passionate about and does your day to day life genuinely reflect that?
40. If you could wave a magic wand and everything was how you want it; how would it be different? (This question is twee but reveals dissatisfactions and goals.)

41. Do you think you have found you life's mission or purpose? Have you answered: why am I here?

NOTE: you may not need to ask them all. Where appropriate get the client to rate the fulfilment from 0-10. 0 = no fulfilment. 10 = total fulfilment. A rating of less than 3 can in some people be enough to trigger anxiety, depression etc.

Quick self-esteem/worth boost for those experiencing addictions.

With some addicts you need to boost their self-worth as we have seen. Although the following is far from all you can do, I offer some concrete ways to get a person, any person, feeling good about themselves without artifice. If you like yourself – you just don't need drugs. It is that simple often. Adapt and use as you wish. I will offer 'deeper insights' to building self-worth in my next book.

Self-esteem/worth boost for addicts script.

(Where you include this in the session is down to you. Only use IF self-worth is an issue – 99% of the time it's not. Deep hypnosis assumed...)

'The thing about building self-worth is that...it's more about re-building it...Everyone is born with self-worth...It's just part of your birth right to ***relax and feel good about yourself, now...*** In fact you have had many moments where you ***feel comfortable being yourself...***You weren't being overly harsh and critical like some sort of never pleased perfectionist judge... Somehow at such moments you ***relax when thinking about yourself and your genuine qualities...***

No one can ever be 100% objective about themselves...You can't know all the things about you that charm others...You can't know them but you can know you have such an effect on many people...Perhaps a specific time springs to mind? You should ***treat yourself kindly...***Why do you have to live up to imaginary ideals that others don't? Some games aren't worth playing.

I know you have compassion for deserving others...I know you have forgiven others for certain things...don't you deserve to ***treat yourself that way, now?***

So you know you aren't perfect! Thank goodness. So you know you aren't Superman/Wonder Woman. Thank goodness. So you know that you are fallible at times. Thank goodness. So you know you made some mistakes. Thank goodness because that's how we all learn. We feel guilt because we care but when we ***learn the lessons*** of an experience you can move on from that...

Is there someone you regard positively and who you really appreciate in your life? Think of the perspective they take with regards to you and ***utilise that position when evaluating yourself...***We need to ***lighten up*** about things sometimes...We need to ***see the funny side...*** We need to know that ***you're fine as you are...You are as good as anyone else*** and the *core* of you knows this!

As I pause I would like it if you could ponder your good qualities...What key images or words associated with those qualities do you need to re-connect to? These will just emanate, bubble up if you like from your far deeper, wiser self... I'll be quiet for 30 seconds as you go through that pleasurable process. *(Do so.)*

Great and having done that...***you are objectively aware of your strengths*** too now, are you not? I know there are things you do very well. *(After each statement pause for a beat.)* I know you have displayed and demonstrated kindnesses...I know you can complete things that need completing...I know that you really know that many people like many things about you...I know people have told you what they appreciate about you...I know you know real right from wrong...I know you care about others' wellbeing...I know you have talents...I know there are times you have been brave...I know you have said the right thing at the right time...I know all this because you are human and you can ***ponder the reality of your true nature...***as I continue to talk...

I had a lady client come to see me once and the problem was she had forgotten how to ***focus on strengths...***but she knew how to do it. You see we can ***learn*** that there are some things that we were wrong about...When that happens we update our knowledge and ***operate from a new more objective map of reality...***If you were to imagine some people you love, talking about you...what kind things might they say? Imagine that you can overhear such a time now...like eavesdropping... Note how much they appreciate you...so that you can ***realistically get a sense of your true worth...***feeling so calm and good about that magical learning...Just ***absorb these understandings...*** *(Give 'em 30 secs or so...)*

What we call 'self-esteem' or 'self-worth' is a series of interconnected feelings...and I would like your most wondrous self to allow a colour that represents all those lovely feelings to bubble up...That's right. Let that colour spread all through you taking your feelings of self-worth to all the places inside that they need to go...Let that colour-feeling ***soothe and melt away doubt*** with loving calm...Let your perception of who you really are re-emerge... Find a way, almost mysteriously, to ***see yourself as you truly are...***As though you have a magical mirror that only reflects reality...

What new insights about yourself can you discover from this more honest perspective? Three people seeing one event take quite different positions...You can't please everyone nor should you try. A real friend can take a 'no' now and again. From this place of ***so much more calm and confidence...***You'll be able to ***appraise yourself fairly***...more and more and more...You were too being too hard on yourself...Now you know it's much better to ***feel genuine self-respect...feel good about yourself...feel proud of your achievements...***You know deep down ***you are a good person...***You know deep down that ***you have worth...***You know deep down that ***you have much to offer...***You can ***act from a place of real strength...***You can ***act from your highest values...You can achieve more than you know...***And what's more you can instantaneously learn to believe that...***all these new beliefs have simply become a part of the deepest roots of YOU!*** Because its time, really time to ***be at peace with yourself, now...***And this is so...'

(This is not overly long or complicated – you are just starting to stimulate new ways of looking at things. You can throw in a future pace etc. or just link this to a future pace when doing another phase of the work. For example – 'See that you over there with very good self-esteem; notice how they are acting etc.')

Traits of the addicted.

I rummaged through ALL my interviews with clients who had any kind of addiction process that made up their problem matrix; even if it only composed a small part of it. I was looking for recurring themes and similarities – this is what I found:

- They are easily affected by group think.
- They perceive they are rebellious.
- They are often single.
- The addiction is threatening their primary relationship.
- They can be any social class.
- They often do the drug etc. in secret.
- They are usually quite intelligent.
- The worst display varying degrees of irresponsibility in wider life.
- They are usually VERY good hypnotic subjects.
- 'Respectable' ladies do lots of drugs! Even mums/moms can be secret crack addicts. No, I don't mean they like anal sex you fiend!

- Some druggies are total degenerates.
- Male addicts perceive drugs as risk taking.
- 99% of those who come to see you genuinely do want help to change. 1% are time wasters – but they they're paying so f**k it. You gotta eat right!?

Drug addiction deprogramming summation.

Let me just refresh your mind as to the core deprogramming principles that help any hypnotist help an addiction client – almost like a check list. Recall the key themes.

Deprogramming protocols that work.

1. Get the client nice and relaxed in hypnosis.
2. Do *thorough* parts work.
3. Diminish positive associations of addiction.
4. Get the client to seriously consider the consequences of their actions: this is long term planning training.
5. Increase negative associations with addiction. (3, 4 and 5 refocus the mind.)
6. Do 'ego boost' work.
7. Use multiple methods of attack. One script alone won't work!
8. Dissociate the client from the habit.
9. Associate client into a future

resourceful self.

10. Build in self-generated good feelings – 'positive feeling entrainment'.

11. Include post hypnotics for future good feelings IF they stay healthy etc.

12. Include withdrawal 'coping mechanisms'.

13. Use time distortion techniques readily yet skilfully.

14. Show the client ways to get genuine needs met through a changed lifestyle.

15. Symbolise/reframe the drug as a parasite, thief etc.

16. Frame addictions as abusive relationships.

17. *Important: credit the client with successful work done.*

Addiction deprogramming working assumptions/maxims.

In no particular order…

- ALL addiction is beatable – you just need the right change patterns in the right sequence: addiction matrices are structurally similar AND yet unique to the individual.

- Drugs abuse the user not the other way around.
- The brain produces all the natural uppers and downers it needs.
- People with addictions become healthy when their needs are met NOW, no matter what crap happened in the past.
- The more someone tries to quit the more likely they are to succeed. Persistence = 'cure'!
- Calm down the client's general arousal levels. Heightened arousal/stress is linked to addictive behaviour.
- Hypnotic addiction deprogramming is about negotiation not bullying.
- Aim for 1 session cures.
- Addiction 'cures' NEVER replace one drug with another – say illegal for legal.
- All 'parts' of a person must be on board to ensure success.
- Parts change behaviours when you offer better alternatives.
- Former 'addicts' tell their friends how

great you are – this equals MONEY!

- Save your client money and he or she will want to ensure you get more of it.
- Addiction clients must unconsciously BELIEVE that change is possible. You might have to install that belief.
- Stress free people are funnier!
- Identify the specific problem matrix of the individual before you – there is no such thing as a generic drug busting session etc.
- The client is responsible for supplying almost ALL motivation – you are responsible for guiding them through precisely the right change process.
- When people feel good naturally they don't need drugs.
- Take the scripts in this book – rework them, rewrite them and mix and match them, switch them around etc. in such a way that you can use all or parts of them to help that specific client. *Your judgement will be the key.*

You have the tools, now go and help as many people as want to be helped. Addiction can be deprogrammed – *fast!*

NOW GO SLAP ADDICTION SILLY!!!

The Rogue Hypnotist wishes you well in all your deprogramming endeavours my Padawan! My book series is almost done:

COMING SOON –

'Hypnotically annihilating anxiety! Penetrating confessions of a Rogue Hypnotist': guess what that's about Einstein!? O.C.D, depression, G.A.D, nervous breakdown recovery, stuttering – we'll cover it all; the 'mysteries' will be revealed for next to nothing. For those readers who have been with me from the start or have read my other books, I thank you for kindly for accompanying me on this amazing journey! I am thrilled so many are getting so much from my books! More than you know...As for the troll haters, you amuse me! Bless your silly-titted hearts! Sense of humour – Get one!

Appendices.

Appendix 1: The irresistible neuroscience induction.

The following is 100% my own invention, based on my extensive research on hypnosis and neuroscience. I wanted to come up with a VERY powerful hypnotic induction; it would be conversational and *irresistible.* In this script we are actively seeking to use language and create activities that seduce the 'hypnotic parts' of the brain. Our prime target for hypnotic 'seduction' is the part of the brain known as the ACC or anterior cingulate cortex. And by the way Dr. Milton Erickson used the term seduction in therapy work. He meant nothing sexual by it. See book 7, 'Escaping cultural hypnosis' for a full discussion on the AAC's fundamental involvement in all hypnotic processes. As outlined in 'Wizards of trance' you can try the following hypno-tricks, not necessary but optional:

- Speak slower than usual.
- Use a rhythmical pattern to your speech: 4-8 words per phrase/sentence. This produces a melody which appeals to the subconscious.
- Make each phrase a separate

statement/suggestion.

- Wait 2-5 seconds at the end of each hypnotic phrase to let ideas sink in, be acted upon by the 'other than conscious processes'.

You might want to experiment with this script with a client on a second session rather than a first or just jump in at the deep end – up to you!

The irresistible neuroscience induction script.

(This script is predominantly a basic pacing and leading script, Ericksonian style – but we are not just pacing external physical manifestations and assumed internal ones of hypnotic trance – **we are assuming knowledge and so pacing *brain activity* etc.** That's VERY powerful pacing – the conscious and unconscious guarding mechanisms hearing so much vague yet descriptive truth go down.)

Close your eyes please... *(Activates alpha waves almost instantly.)* Just become aware of your body...Do not try to ***relax it...***just notice its reality... *(Beginning focus on somatosensory functions.)* That's fine...just gently, gradually ***re-focus your awareness*** of the outer world for ***your inner, subjective world, now...***

There is a part that breathes for you...so that

you don't have to be aware of it. We notice the ***rise and fall*** of clouds on sunny daze/days... *(Pacing breathing.)* That's a nice thing to ***feel secure*** about isn't it? ***A part*** *(command – 'dissociate')* is aware of your pulse...Your heartbeat...Its rhythm...A part is aware of sensations anywhere on your skin at any time...it needs to be or not...A part monitors internal feeling too...Temperatures are noticed... from time to time...Warmings and coolings...An awareness of balance and movement and ***growing stillness...***

Listening, there is a part of you that can gradually ***lessen its waking state*** function... That's it. A rain drop clings to a leaf before it suddenly let's go...While ***resting*** you can knowingly ***reflect*** on things – when ***you're in hypnosis*** you're learning in a different way... And wondering...what you'll be learning... because, I am talking to your emotional brain, if you like...

Can you ***imagine*** a pear and an apple in two separate picture frames, side by side? Good. Now simply push those two pictures far away in your mind...and ***relax...*** *(Overload spatial channels...)*

Can you imagine from your own point of view trying to pat your head and rub your tummy all at once...while you hop on the spot? *(Goal: to overload the executive function. Pause a beat..)*

Can you just get the sense of a map of your body?

Did you ever ***focus so intently*** on something that you just ***forget about what is going on around you*** (?)

Something different happens...inside, when you...***follow instructions,*** does it not? I know there is a part of you initiating, inhibiting, regulating and consolidating possible response sets and potentials...***that activity can lessen then stop*** for a while... *(Shutting down 'contention scheduling'.)*

There is a part that recognises faces, feelings, their interpretation, subtle communications... *(Activating other than conscious processes.)*

There have been times when you were reliant on instruction in order to gain independence, were their not? A suggestion is something you can ***choose to act*** upon...and there is no need for a certain type of awareness here...

There is a part I am communicating with...it is intuitive, rapid, dynamic: it can ***select different ideas and meaningfully interpret them...***

Are you aware of any feelings? What is it about my voice that attracts your attention most? Where else is your awareness drifting to? Where on your body, where you skin touches a piece of clothing...does you intent ***focus*** upon naturally? What positive chains of thought do you associate to ***calmness***? *(Turning on the Primary Attentional System.)*

There is ***apart*** that readies itself to solve problems...You can expect that nothing that happens here will be unexpected...- just the expectancy is enough...it has the power of ***insight...***I would like to thank all parts of you for their cooperation... *(Assumed!)*

Can you recall an everyday, routine habit you do without effort? ***The part that processes that on your part can begin to predominate*** your information processing, ***now.*** Or if you prefer the ***hypnotic part can light up*** while another dampens...What if you could ***switch off that evaluative mechanism, now...***

You see, when you are ***learning from someone*** with desirable knowledge...a particular function needs to ***stop chattering and commenting...***inside your mind, now... in order to ***absorb relevant information*** easily. In this changing state as you ***gently slide into hypnosis...***an image or images, memories that please you can come to mind...

In trance, you can examine, express, learn from, assimilate and reject safely and privately... The gift of your imagination is in part its ability to help you...***find new responses to old challenges...***

Can you recall a time you were feeling something nice with your hands? That's it, just get the sense of it: vivid or not...What did it feel like to manipulate with your hands? *(A beat or so...)*

Once you've done that, can you recall or ***imagine*** a time when you were eating something out of this world delicious? Get the sense of that now...The feel of its texture and amazing mouth-watering taste in your mouth... All your taste buds alive and thrilled at the experience...That's right. *(A beat...)*

And can you recall or imagine an entrance to a shelter...? I don't know when or where that is... you do...Can you imagine, when you are ready, going inside that shelter...? If you haven't already and ***feeling so protected and safe*** there...lovely...Enjoy this place. *(A beat...)*

Now, can you recall a very long word you learnt? Can you hear that in your mind – feel that pen or pencil as you wrote it...Or tried to... Perhaps it was confusing at first or easy...I remember hearing the word

'Supercalifragilisticexpialidocious'...Now, that's a mouthful...Any words like that can spring to mind...See the letters in your mind if that helps...Good...These words here are important... and can be processed and prioritised similarly... now...

(The above visualising etc. section accesses the hardwired linguistic priorities of the mind's needs. That is, it uses linguistic imagery linked to primary prioritised brain channels for survival; see my book 'Wizards of trance' for details.)

As you can be absolutely certain that you're not sure the old ways were best, now. That's the way...And as ***that happens...***one hemisphere of your brain might begin to predominate even more...Certainly certain alterations can and will occur...You could notice states...qualities... changes...and it knows how to ***do this... now...***on your behalf...And there could be pleasant changes in your ***focus*** meanwhile... because ***your brain acts differently in hypnosis...***than it usually does when you're awake...and when you ***sleep and dream...*** Certain things I say will appeal to differing parts of you...In fact your ***brainwaves alter appropriately*** during this process...Certain functions dampen their activity for a while... The good thing is we all have an internal survival mechanism for ***acting upon essential***

suggestions... *(Activating openness to unconscious genetic/hardwired pro-survival suggestions template/s.)*

The part that checks, monitors and analyses – looks for feedback, makes choices and forms strategies...observes whether goals are achieved and waking needs met, can ***rest easy*** for a bit...take a pause and reflect in a new way...as it processes certain information in a new way... *(Asking the ACC – anterior cingulate cortex, to modulate its function.)* the back of it is more active than the front...a certain region switches or modulates its function...Your usual awareness can ***go elsewhere*** in a natural way...***in this altered state, now...***

You can gain access to new choices because ***you are so deeply relaxed...***You are free here to ***set unhelpful habits aside...***You are free here to ***experiences certain re-associations*** that helpfully happen, independently and unconsciously, now... Internal inter-communication changes happen in order to ***facilitate creative change...*** The way you process information changes pleasurably...You become more attuned to the powerful inner reality...of the input of your visualising capacity...to create better, more functional and successful hypnotic realities... that you can learn from to ***live more happily in waking life...*** *(Deep hypnotic relaxation* *allows the 'innovative part' to start to work spontaneously.)*

And the part that does such things is listening... it always was...It can assist you in ***feeling nice feelings, more often...***That's nice to know, isn't it? Hypnosis is like a word massage that ***eases away*** all past unnecessary tension, now...The creative part of you is more than capable...of helping you ***find improved paths*** to satisfy a positive intent...Better things can be associated to during this, and in this place...this quiet place of peace...because in life we can metaphorically - get lost...and when that happens we need to ***listen to a helpful guide...***so that you can ***find your true way again...***

You see, what you are experiencing now...is not usual wakefulness...You have confirmed this for yourself...How does it feel to ***be wakefully unawake?*** The tense manner in which you had held those muscles ready for action is not required here...But you mustn't ***fully surrender*** to this until ***you're ready...***In this altered state of consciousness...YOU can ***be at peace...***In this state you ***experience an intense relaxation...***a narrow focus...yet a broader perspective...And you have a velvety strong desire to ***go deeper still...***Small subtle shifts and ***drifting*** can create great progress for you...Lend you ears to some good ideas...

in this fluid state...Between once place and another you can...make new understandings... new awarenesses can captivate you...as ***you introspect*** in just the right way...An aware silent slumber...into lovely unconscious oblivion...Aware that there are other ways to be aware...Calmly relaxing as the calming relaxes... Difficulties will not be solved with the past methods...Solutions will not be found by continually doing the same thing...Nor will ***you succeed in your session's aims...***through more of the same. And there is a truth in that for the deeper mind to ponder...

A particular part of you, which is ***listening*** to me...at some level controls your relaxation response, now, to certain communications offered...Soothing, rocking, gentling, a softening – all is well here...With kindness to self...with compassion for mistakes...with a knowledge that you can **heal...**amazing transformations have been known to occur in a very private way...And processes far beyond my understanding undertake such eventualities on your behalf...The state you seek can be found spontaneously in joyous ways when, in the nicest...safest way only...***you joyfully lose yourself temporarily*** in a crowd, say at a concert...or a sports or artistic event. Exactly!

There are times when ***you're unconscious mind plays the dominant role, now.***

Happens when a person can ***become thoroughly absorbed*** in a book... *(Absorption module follows...)* when you ***enter a trance*** as you socialise...as you ***feel fascination while learning*** something worthwhile...Your ability to feel 100% absorbed in this process or any other is natural...In sports we call it – ***finding your zone...***You're being, ***in the zone, now...***When writing you ***enter it...***When you need to ***ignore irrelevant distractions...***When were you last really involved in something pleasurable? Have you ever been engaged in something fully? What's it like when you ***feel utterly engrossed*** in something? *(A beat after each question.)* Do you have a consuming passion? Have you felt wrapped up in a person or event? Have you noticed times when ***your attention is fixed?*** Feeling head over heels in love is one example...A time you were ***deep*** in thought or imagination another...Really into something, someone, attractive, captivating... ***preoccupied, inside...now...***You are looking for and finding unique ways to ***effortlessly immerse yourself in this...***And the best thing is it feels so good to do so...

Changes in the environment can ***trigger trance states...***Changes of circumstance can ***elicit trance...***These modulations of experience create ***changes in appropriate behavioural expression.*** Such as when we listen to great music in which...***your***

perception of time somehow alters... *(Altering the brain's 'time clicks'.)* Because we have a certain intent, you ***let this occur...***Like when you ***go with the flow...***Some have suggested your inner clocks ticks more slowly... Or another part is too busy to notice the ticks... Others that time can speed up. Who knows? You're deeper mind knows just the right response that would serve your highest intent... And it's not for me...to say to you...what that might be...Here your perception of time is flexible and plastic...It is usually accompanied by an unawareness of certain events...and a heightened awareness of others. But the nice things is that we all need to ***daydream*** from time to time...

Certain times have pleasurably stirred your emotions...one in particular, perhaps several might come to mind...and lead you ***deeper, deeper, deeper...***Positive ideas and emotions can be healthily contagious as it were...In a place where ***you are deeply suggestible, now...***This is a place where you can really ***learn from your best self...***In this place ***suggested ideas can become immediate acts...***Words and other symbols can and do have a powerful effect in hypnotic trance...

For example soon I'll click my fingers 3 times. With each click you ***go 10 times deeper*** into an amazing state of hypnosis, deeper than you imagine possible, possibly...

CLICK! *(Take you time...)*
CLICK!
CLICK! It can be that easy...

Here, external vision gives way to internal vision...In this state input is received, processed, acted upon via certain words and your imaginative response – some people find as you go deeper into hypnosis you can ***'think' in images...***Your brain can ***newly pattern match*** when appropriate...when it would help ***satisfy your needs best of all as a total personality*** to helpful ideas and act on them... You are capable of greater deeds than you consciously know...

Have you ever experienced something playfully joyous, unexpected? A delightful surprise? On such occasions a part of you does ***switch your focus of attention rapidly...***You might notice changes in my speech...patterns......too......... Symbols, geometric shapes, patterns, that you associate with ***going deeper*** or just positive change can come to mind easily...That's it! I'll be quiet for 30 seconds while that process occurs... *(Do so...)*

In this state the unexpected appears quite expected after all. There is no risk in ***safe change...***Imagine an old time hypnotist's watch is swinging before you...and it slows... right......down.........inside...You can ***generate your own experience, now.*** You can attend to this and not that. In this state you can ***have moments of inspiration*** that positively affect your waking reality. Let me tell you a story... when ***you are in a good mood*** your creativity is enhanced...A happy brain is far better at solving problems than a stressed one. You can use insight. When you ***feel better about yourself and life,*** unconscious problem solving occurs. A part of you modulates this fun-ction and I would like to thank it for you! *(The ACC!)* About that story...it's called, 'The Man in a mood!'

The man in a mood metaphor.

Now there may be relations to things you have not yet considered...in stories the elusive may be illuminated...When one's mode of attention is more 'global', access is open to non-usual, un-habitual associations. Differing meanings that were distant may be integrated...That which was weaker may become much stronger, now. Here you can switch between possible solutions and find the best. Associations in one context may not be a good as others in another...shifts and selections of ***a new solution path*** can and do occur...pre-potent responses can be set aside as new potencies are discovered...and adhered to...

When ***you are profoundly relaxed...***there is a greater scope of possible meanings available when ***you feel pleasant emotions*** that allow you to ***gain access to healthier sets of associations,*** emotions, impulses, urges, tendencies can ***become redirected...***With that in mind...

Once upon a time there was a man...a man in a mood...he couldn't even remember why he was so cross...he couldn't even remember why he was in such a state...he couldn't even remember why he felt so bad...Everything was black and white...wrong and right...He deserved to feel that way! The whole world and all the people in it were to blame...

And as he wandered in his fog of rage he didn't notice that he had wandered into a wood...It was the kind of forest where the trees were so densely packed...that he couldn't see the forest for the trees as they say...And whichever way he turned and tried to get out of that wood...he got more and more lost...And his mood got worse and worse...and he got more and more lost...It was as though he had been going around and around in circles getting nowhere in particular...which did not make him feel better at all...

He grew so cross at everything and nothing all at once that he kicked a log...He stubbed his foot so bad that he hopped around...And to top it all, it started to rain and he had no coat...It was at that point that he tripped and rolled down the hill, ***all the way down...***

At the bottom of the slope he looked around and saw a beautiful pool amongst the trees... Not quite a lake and far bigger than a puddle... So he brushed himself down and drew closer... He sat down and looked out at the water...As he looked at the reflections on the water's surface...the sight of the kingfisher darting to and fro, he began to ***feel a natural calm returning...***The way the sunlight pierced through the canopy of green leaves above... The smell of the air and wood about him...He listened to all the sounds – Birdsong...Squirrels squeaking...Things unseen in the undergrowth... And as ***that mind relaxes along with the body...***His perspective began to change...

Here, from this place, things didn't seem quite so bad...He remembered stubbing his toe and falling and it made him smile, then laugh...And as he sat there...***absorbing this experience...***without any effort, ideas came to mind of how to solve a problem...It was as though he had lightened up in this place...He found that when you ***feel in a better mood...*** Obstacles don't seem so impassable or is that impossible? Because although he didn't know it consciously...a part of him solves problems using insight, intuition, connecting associations in new ways and more...and when that happens, now...he found his way out of the wood...And ***feeling good*** helped...

There are many states of mind and body... some help us get our needs met...and others may be a bit too much once...you ***get things in their proper perspective...***And seeing the world as it is rather than through the dimmed spectacles of ***old moods that can melt away so easily...***to leave you with solutions, as that part of you solves your problems unconsciously, now...And the key is – ***lighten up and relax...*** and the way, just the right way or ways have a funny way of just presenting themselves, sometimes when you least suspect it. And knowing, really knowing this is so can make you ***feel much better about things,*** without quite knowing why? That's a nice kind of knowledgeable ignorance, isn't it?

(This metaphor aims to get the ACC working properly – solving problems through insight and not pointless and stressful rumination loops. Carry on with change work of choice. If you felt a bit hypnotised reading the script you can WAKE UP, now...)

Appendix 2: Rogue's hypnotic powerful induction script + deepeners for addictions.

As you may not have read my other books, I am giving you an entirely new induction as an option with addiction work. It is easy to use and adapt as you see fit.

The Rogue Hypnotist's 1st session hypnotic induction.

(What follows is a slight variant of what I pretty much use as a first session induction with all clients 100% of the time. It is 'field tested' – it works really well barring a few imbeciles – I'd say it's 99.9% effective statistically which ain't bad. You can use it for any type of work you like but I have tailored it for addiction work: just use your common sense. For details on language and techniques within it, examine my first 4 books.)

Step 1: Induction begins.

Okay...Just close your eyes...Good...And all I want you to do is to start paying attention to your breathing...That's it...In...and out... *(Pace to the actual breathing phases...)* It's now time to ***feel growing comfort...***And as you simply ***focus*** on your breathing...Can you just take a deep breathe in for me and hold it...Great...And slowly release that breathe...That's it. Because breathing out is a ***relaxing*** motion...And one more time please...Deep breath in and hold it *(I do this myself with the client...)*! And slowly release that breath and ***relax a bit more...*** When you relax on an out breath...***your comfort only increases...***That's right! *(Look out for signs of trance manifestation and verbally reward it.)*

Now, you don't have to do anything at all... Nowhere to go...Nothing to do as you...***go into trance*** and you ***become absorbed...***Noticing any pleasant sensations, processes, experiences as you...***go inside now...***Because all you need to do is just allow certain things to happen... Just turn your attention inwardly...and do an internal body check...Scanning that body *('that' body – implies it's separate, encouraging 'dissociation')* so that you notice and experience any responses of that body to these fascinating words and be able to ***enjoy how pleasant this make you feel*** as you ***feel, really feel a kind of growing comfort.*** That's it.

<u>*Step 2: Deeper inner absorption.*</u>

Imagine breathing through your solar plexus, that's right. Now imagine a colour that makes you ***feel very calm...***and comfortable, now... Allow a wave of that colour of comfort to begin to spread from the top of your head ***all the***

way down to the tips of your toes...All of your muscles becoming softer, letting go now...as you notice any sounds that you hear...any words that I say...anything and everything allows you to ***drift off...***You may hear the sound of my voice going with you. Only pleasant thoughts... pleasant images...perhaps one relaxing memory can drift through your mind...as you fully ***enter this state...***

You don't have to open your eyes or talk...let me do the talking for a while...You don't have to understand consciously...your beliefs...your unconscious beliefs are all that matters...And which part is most comfortable? Funny to find ***all feels well...***On occasion it can be very good and pleasant enjoying ***letting go...***of certain directions and controls to permit unconscious autonomous (independent) processes to take over...

Step 3: Prime ideas of success, conversational deepeners, enhanced inner focus.

You may be ***wondering*** what will shift and change first...And you can easily use all your powers of inner focus ensuring ***you will achieve all you desire from this session*** without knowing how you did it consciously... How much further into trance and hypnosis can you really go? Enjoy feeling more and more wonderfully comfortable as you ***go deeper***

inside...You could notice words and notice noticing words. And the deeper you go the more wonderful you feel and the more wonderful you feel the deeper...you can go, now! *(Say this with 'profound' intent.)* That's right.

As we continue you can ***hear/here my voice...***and other times it may seem quiet and distant...and at other times it doesn't matter if you can hear it at all...because you can allow a deeper part of you to ***hear all you need to hear, NOW.*** You can't turn your ears off! And you know that you are the one who is in control as we make amazing changes...And anyone can ***know the fullness of comfort each day...*** And you can follow your own associative processes to these words...Like the word - ***'comfort'*** and follow where it takes you, ***now.***

Step 4: Permissive/non-challenge eye challenge 'test' and metaphorical deepener.

Your eyelid muscles can feel so very relaxed that your ***eyes*** easily remain ***closed***... *(Subliminal command – 'eyes closed!')* And as they do...you ***feel even more absorbed*** in pleasant processes...Each out breath helps melts away past tension...which floats away into the distance, like storm clouds melting...fading away into the distance...like on sunny days, guaranteeing your success. Knowing - you don't have to do those things you once did. And as a person's mind develops other awarenesses – the body can ***rest.*** And you don't have to move...unless that movement brings you more of that which you wish.

Step 5: (optional) Linguistic expectation deepener.

(This is a sneaky way to do a challenge test that doesn't seem like a challenge – see 'Forbidden hypnotic secrets' for the mechanics...)

In a moment not now but soon I will simply say one hypnotic word...This hypnotic word is SO mighty that when I say it ***you will fall instantly into a very deep hypnotic trance*** that will feel lovely, okay? Are you ready? *(Do not await response...go!)* Good. Ah but wait... Before we do that, can you answer this question? But only in your own mind for yourself...Can you recall the exact year you first did x? *(X being a memorable event – first day at school, first kiss, first time you saw fireworks etc.; stay away from trauma! Give them 2-3 seconds and then hit them with...)*

'SLEEP!' *(Said forcefully, stage hypnosis style!)* All...the way down! That's it.

Step 6: Shrinking numerals deepener.

(This is a variation of an old deepener that uses basic visualisation and symbology; numbers are implicitly linked with logic – if they 'vanish' so does logical thinking, by implication...)

See a flat surface in your mind's eye...Trust what your subconscious automatically offers... Soon, not yet but very soon you'll see a set of numbers ***going down...***from 10-1 appear on that surface...

When I count down from 10-1 those numerals will alter to match the figures I am counting ***downward now, all...the way...down.*** And as they head down to 1 they'll get smaller and smaller! As though by magic! Hypnosis magic, now! But before they even reach 5 they'll have shrunk so teeny-weeny that they would have vanished already! *(Sound a bit surprised!)* When this happens...you will have already ***become deeply absorbed and enthralled*** by ***a state of deep hypnotic trance, now...*** Deeper than you might have imagined was possible.

Okay – you ready? Here we go! 10, 9...getting smaller and smaller...***going down...***8 – more immersed...Where are they going? 7 – more so of that! 6 – almost there! *'5!'* Not a sign!

AWOL! Disappeared! ***Blissful...oblivion, now!*** Absent! *(These are subtle, jokey commands for consciousness to go by-by!)* But that's a nice feeling you *are* left with, is it not?

Step 7: Colour symbols as deepeners.

In a moment, not this very moment but soon enough - this will happen...I am just going to say the names of certain shades of colours... You'll see them as I say them...As I say all 3 of them, at the moment I do say them, you will ***experience deeper hypnosis, deeper trance, now...***With each specific colour I say you can ***become progressively more comfortable...become progressively more relaxed and receptive...become more and more hypnotised, now...***You will enjoy the whole process I lead you through very much.

With each colour I say your expectation of certain success is heightened. If I say the word - 'intensify' that blissful feeling of deep hypnosis can but strengthen...If I say the words - 'hypnotic enchantment' – you find a way to spontaneously ***experience a level of hypnotic trance 50 times deeper,*** more profound, beautifully relaxing and anything else your deepest mind wants you to...All this will ***begin*** with the first colour feeling I say; if it hasn't already? If not sooner than that! Are you ready now? *(Rhetorical – continue!)* **SKY BLUE!** Go down and ***intensify*** that state! And that feels really good doesn't it? *(Give them about 5 secs to bathe in it.)*

GRASS GREEN! Double that and ***intensify*** it more and more...And that pleasurable state you can bathe and float in feels amazing doesn't it! Look at all the pleasure your mind can naturally make available to you...and there is a lesson in this. *(Give them about 5 secs to bathe in it.)* And one last time for luck – make the feelings really good!

AUTUMN RED ! Autumn: the time of CHANGE! Deeper and deeper - ***intensify*** this set of feelings! Quadruple the pleasure of your ***hypnotic enchantment, now!!!*** That's it – just indulge yourself in that much better state. A facilitating state. *(Give them about 5 secs to bathe in it.)*

And anyone could wonder, really wonder how they could...***have nice feelings inside anyway*** and ***a sense of deepest comfort*** and keep them permanently too...A part rests; another part is heightened in power! With that hypnotic reality in mind...

Step 8: 'Master command' installation!

(Say with authority and expect 'magic' to happen!)

From this very second on...all sounds...all voices...inside and out...create an ease in your ***focus on my voice, now!*** At some level or just ***drift off*** somewhere nice...You ***follow meaningful words...***ideas that help only more easily...Nothing that happens, that I do, bother you in any way, shape or form...Whatever I say can promptly occur, can exclusively become your new total reality no matter if it sounds funny, brand new, or very different! You can experientially ***know what I say!*** You can think ***what I suggest you do!*** You can ***believe what I tell you to believe!*** And you can ***feel that which I suggest powerfully*** with every part of your being! When I say ***you can do it,*** whatever it is, you can ***do it*** and you can know that you can know you can. Only with regards to the matters we are working with obviously*.

And now...everything that occurs merely takes you ***deeper and deeper...***Bodily changes and actions...sensations and awarenesses...You can ***go deeper and deeper than ever before, now!***

(This section is an indirect super-command-suggestion, saying in effect – 1. Anything from

*now on is defined as 'hypnotic'. 2. Think, feel, believe, act and know what I suggest to you from this instant on. *This may get resistance BUT I follow it up with a safety feature suggestion which says, only do as I say with regards to the hypnotherapy problems etc. Thus they are ensured they won't become my mind control bitch!)*

Step 9: The ultimate hypnotic trance tunnel!

Very soon I will say the word 'intensify' 5 times; each time I say it you will drift closer and closer to the ultimate depths of hypnotic trance that you can unconsciously experience...After the 5th time I say that hypnotic word and follow it with the phrase ***'deepest hypnotic enchantment*'*** you will enter the most incredible...penetrating...secret...phenomenal hypnotic experience you never even conceived of up till now... *(*This phrase is still an operative deepener from earlier on. Sneaky!)* It will be stunning and blissfully surprising...The most blissful state of hypnotic trance ever!

It all starts when you...imagine a beautiful tunnel that leads to a bright ending off in that alluring distant view. You know you ***want and need to go there...***You realise with the certain prospect of realistic joy and trust that you need to reach the end of that tunnel...You can run, sprint, fly, float – it's all up to you...This is your experience...No one can tell you how to ***go into the most profound state of hypnosis possible...***

As I say the hypnotic words you approach the distant healing light that takes you beyond your former perceived limitations...to the depths of the potential wellsprings of who you really are and are destined to be...Ready? We are never really ready...you just need to be ready enough! Here we go!

Intensify! Approach that light in your preferred way! Nearer and nearer...deeper and deeper!

Intensify! Even nearer – and there is a bliss in knowing that ***positive change is coming*** and that although I am your guide YOU are the author of the change and life you desire and deserve!

Intensify! – Closer than ever before: wonderful feelings like you've never felt coursing through you, making ***you feel amazing!*** You are almost where you need to be...You are almost beyond that which once held you back...So near, so very near...Feel your motivation to change

Intensify! Here...You are on the

threshold...A feeling of utter ***peace of mind, clarity of purpose and firm conviction*** flood through you, from the deepest parts of your being! Almost there...Almost there... Reaching the tunnel's end! Almost...there! And the healing light magnifies 100 fold and fills you with ***awesome feelings of transcendent bliss, now!***

Intensify! *(When you reach the climax you can quieten the voice; this is the opposite of what is expected and so dramatic! Pause a beat!)* You have passed over the past hurdles! ***You are free*** of mental chains of any kind! You are out of reach of that! You have advanced just as you wished - through the illusory barriers! Into an inner realm of ***deepest...hypnotic... enchantment...*** *NOOOOOOOOOO-OOOOOOOOOOOOOW!!!!!!!*

Enjoy that unique, private experience! Let it go now! Let it all go! The doors are open! Let this embrace and consume you! Ride that experience where it needs to take you...And the deeper you knows just what I mean...Let the wondrous feelings emanate within you and out beyond you! That's it!

Feel your power to change positively now!

Remain comfortably at whatever level you want and need...***In deepest hypnosis...In deepest trance...In this changing state...*** And the part that plans and questions need pay no mind but may ***rest blissfully*** as the ***healing*** process takes place...It will return more strengthened and powerful than ever at the end of this session...

AND NOW...I am speaking to the deepest part of who you really are...I am speaking to the deepest YOU, now!

Step 10: (Optional) Woodland stroll metaphor deepener.

(This is an imagery based deepener...)

As you...***let yourself go deeper comfortably*** in whatever way you're unconscious mind now, wishes...And as you ***breathe hypnotically...*** on each gentle exhale...you find a rhythm that takes you onward...You can ***feel the deep... hypnotic...relaxation*** beginning to soothe... spread throughout all the parts of your body. That's right...

A lot of people like to go out and ***relax*** in the forest, in woodland, amongst the trees. Nature is inherently ***relaxing*** to humans... I know a person can enjoy getting back to nature almost as though ***you're resetting***

things, naturally...and smelling the pleasant smells anyone finds there and ***hearing*** the wind in the trees perhaps and ***my voice*** can be heard like that, *(hypnotic run on/code – 'hearing my voice')* like the wind in the trees...

I'm going to say some things now...but they really won't be about what they seem to be about...because that's not what you want to ***hear now*** is it? As I talk...you can be ***feeling comfortable,*** you can be ***feeling so soothed...***paying some kind of any attention at some level of awareness...***feeling peaceful...***As I can talk about northern forests...that have to stand tall in the world ***feeling still and peaceful...***despite the elements...And the majesty of mountains can look and ***feel so still...***that's a unique thing to talk about...It might make a person curious to ***learn;*** it's funny to think about a forest with feelings: isn't it a puzzle to you?

During this...hypnotic...process...in response to a certain order of words...significant chains of positive memories...may be pleasurably re-associated to...as there are times when we naturally...***don't think or question...***So you can wonder, just wander how you will really learn to ***change at a far deeper level...*** using your imagination to plastically play with ideas and images...that...it's a cold bitter winter, the trees are like silent sentinels in the barren snow-covered landscape, even the bushes are very ***still inside...***No noise but maybe the muffled fall of falling snow...which can make for a ***feeling of comfort and pleasure*** as the forest changes and reveals its true self in a new way...during the healing warmth of the spring, the season of renewal...And those tall as tall trees can ***calmly*** watch over the magical landscape.

A part can ***know such natural stillness,*** can it not? For anyone deeply knows that we can all ***ignore certain inappropriate urges and desires...***at certain times, unconsciously or to pay attention to other things. It just happens.... effortless, now...To do things in the old way is difficult then impossible...You don't dress for winter in spring...We know weather is uncontrollable...and the great and noble trees of the wood like to ***feel totally unaffected*** by the weight of the world. The forest makes it through all of the passing difficulty of a life's unfolding discovery...does it not? Heavy snows must thaw at some time...Nothing lasts forever...Unmoved...And the sun begins to rise in such a blissful, warm and cosy way on spring mornings with ***a feeling of complete tranquillity, now...***

The spring weather makes the forest, ***live with native feelings of pleasure and satisfaction...now...***Life returns. The look of a person strolling through a spring wood is one of ***total serenity, now...***Out here...it's funny how ***some distance makes certain things seem small.*** And the things that once controlled us can't bother <u>*you*</u> at all! Leaves grow back as they do...basking in ***feeling so comfortable*** in the spring sunshine...Gone are the ways of the old and cold winter as insects/bugs begin to dance on the plants... animals renew their number...I wonder if the plants and the trees can, you know, ***feel, really feel a kind of deep-rooted comfort and happiness now...***And if ***there is a natural stillness as you feel rested here...*** That means ***there's no more old troubles...*** things can change, they do, they have, they will...All the problems of the past feel like ***they've been somehow overcome...***and everything is looking better each day.

And you now ***feel so nice inside*** with such a pleasant sensation and you ***feel so happy*** and ***feel profound peace...***Just there and everywhere...anywhere you need it...and natural changes change perceptions...Ask yourself: what is natural? What is naturally good? The deepest you was born knowing. So that things can't pile up in the former way...like snow that fell until ***you find ways to clear certain things away*** before it became a problem...

Your creativity can always help ***you solve a***

problem unconsciously...It seems, suddenly, that everything really is growing better in all directions. And now, smell the pleasant fragrances in the air. Hear attractive sounds and ***go deeper...***into that restful place within... Anyone can taste the deliciousness of the new life that is forming all around you...

Some say of all Mother Nature's or God's creations if you prefer...the trees especially are so happy...They are strong, deep-rooted and solid...yet they have flexibility too...they may absorb that which enriches them...and ***feel so nice*** gazing upon the summer beauty of their seemingly brand-new woodland; yet it is still the same place. It's time to see what you can *really* do, testing limits and breaking through... you suddenly realise – ***you're free!*** Only those illusions had imprisoned you...And then there's those gorgeous, vivid summer sunsets...that are so colourful, beautiful and rich...and it is precisely at such moments that you ***feel totally alive*** that they make ***you feel so happy...***without knowing why.

On certain journeys we know...we say to ourselves...'I'm never going back!' ***The past is in the past!*** Ah! Let it go, let all that – go! You stand there strong! It is as though a new dawn has dawned upon you! The joys of natural things within express themselves in delightful ways...They make the forest ***feel re-***

energised and composed...That sky turns pink, amber, purple, gold, peach, yellow, violet hazes. The woods are engulfed by a velvety blue haze, as though enchanted...The sky above becomes a brilliant starry, starry night. The grandeur of the Milky Way dazzles you with awe! And yet through all these changes the northern forest is ***so peaceful and still, naturally...***And that's a nice place to visit from time to time, is it not?

You can always ***reconnect to this potential...***You are at one with yourself, here... And to whatever degree that is right...certain appropriate changes, learnings and understandings made here will remain with you at a very deep level, now...

(With this deepener we are idea priming/seeding, using metaphors: good feelings, ideas of natural change, the spontaneous nature of effortless change when the time is right etc. Begin with change work of choice...)

Appendix 3: Withdrawal protocol from 'Powerful hypnosis' + bonus sentence*.

This is from 'Powerful hypnosis' BUT I have added two new punchy lines to boost its effectiveness. It works with all addictions that involve drugs that are smoked, snorted etc. EXCEPT for heroin addiction which is more complicated. You don't need it with porn.

Handling physiological withdrawal script.

Part 1: Suggestions to minimise withdrawal reactions.

There may be a very small period of time when you may experience mild physiological withdrawal, there might not but there might be. As your body cleanses itself of those past toxins. But the **subconscious** can **minimise these** *(hypnotic code)* as much as is possible. So that you still ***feel good, sleep well, concentrate easily, feel calm and focused*** with ***no sense of grief at all,*** *(addicts can feel grief at 'losing' the drug – stop that)* as much as is humanly possible.

Part 2: Time distortion.

Whilst the body gets rid of old toxins, ***determined to succeed*** during this short time frame that passes so quickly, *(say this quickly)* before you know it they are gone and you ***feel totally great and fully healthy.***

Your subconscious mind is in charge of your perception of time at any time, it can compress and expand this sense of time passing. If withdrawals, urges or cravings arise they will pass so quickly yet naturally that before you know it ***they are gone completely.*** Trust you have all the resources required within you – desire, determination, toughness, *(say this line and the next with emphasis and meaning!)* endurance and willpower so strong...to get through this tiny amount of time *(emphasise the word – tiny! Make it sound tiny...)* in the grand total of your life *(stretch out the word grand in contrast to – 'graa-aand total...')* knowing those only temporary passing feelings remind you how important it is to ***be fully healthy,*** a non-smoker/free and normal etc. not an ex-smoker etc., always keeping in mind your goals.

Part 3: Snapping a client out of a withdrawal trance.

You can ***focus externally on your goals and activities.*** You ***easily maintain an external focus when you need it.**** Trust that your subconscious will aid you powerfully in all your efforts, now. *(*These two new sentences stop the client going into 'withdrawal' trance, which* *can happen. Nicotine withdrawal does make some people find it harder to focus externally – deal with that.)*

Appendix 4: Exduction – the wake up procedure.

There are several of these in my other books: I'll give you my favourite one here, adapt it as needed…

Generic exduction procedure.

Part 1: Places in the mind and amnesia module.

All these positive ideas and changes have been placed in that place within where you know things to be true. Things like the sun sets, that you know how to breathe. Those old, outdated ways have gone to that place where you place things that were true but no longer are – you knew certain people, you went to school and then it all changed. The certainty of your success is permanently stored in that place where you know, really know that ***amazing changes have already occurred, now…***

You don't have to remember, the important things is to have certain experiences naturally recorded in your mind. Their presence has been and will be of service to you. It's nice to know they are there, unconsciously, now…

Part 2: Post hypnotics.

(These just save you time so I advise you use 'em.)

If you ever want me to help you in the future all I will have to say is ***'DEEP SLEEP!'*** *(etc.)* Only within the context of a hypnosis session obviously and you will instantly re-enter a state of trance and hypnosis 50 times deeper than the one you have experienced easily and quickly.

Part 3: Awakening process.

Okay, I am now going to count from 1 – 5 and on 5 ***everything I have said in this hypnotic session will remain with you at a subconscious level...***Only growing stronger every second of each day of your amazing, more fun-filled life! Enabling you to continue being the confident, happier, healthier, more relaxed calm, confident and loving non-smoker/person who is free and normal *(etc.)* with ***precisely the right mindset, now,*** to achieve your positive, healthy and realistic goals.

Your subconscious aids you in all your efforts. Your poise is good, sense of self-worth returned. That person you have now become, and always really were deep inside, and will continue to be from this moment forward – only building on your success.

On 1 – Realising now that you will awaken every morning and after this session with an inner warm glow of confidence, a renewed optimism for life that just radiates from you and others notice it!

On 2 – Noticing how much better you feel, how proud you feel about yourself for allowing yourself to overcome challenges that you once had that now no longer bother you – it's as if your mind and body have been magically purified! And your conscious self can relax in the trusting knowledge that ***these new habits operate automatically and unconsciously, now.***

3 – All unnecessary relaxation now leaving the body! Lighter and brighter! Almost as though you now realise that a huge weight has been lifted from your shoulders! ***You feel free!*** When ***you wake up in a few moments time*** you will have an overwhelming feeling of being very happy, feeling alert and full of vitality and energy that you'll want to express!

4 – More aware of your body and room around you, aware of noises – normal waking feelings now returning to every muscle group and cell that needs to ***feel wide awake!*** You can

forget to remember what you can remember to forget! All changes made and locked in! Your breathing returns to normal waking breathing! You ***feel clear and fresh*** throughout mind and body! Totally re-energised! Open your eyes on

'5!'

That's it, you're done. *(Which is a suggestion.)*

Appendix 5: 'After care'.

One of the first marijuana addicts I treated said to me – 'What about aftercare?' I thought – 'What about 'aftercare'?' But she was right. This is how you address that topic…

- Let them know you are always available if they need help.
- Tell them to see what happens – if the effects last for 2-3 weeks that usually means that they are doing fine and dandy. Only a life stressor might derail things, not always, but if it does tell the client not to blame themselves.
- Say, 'If I don't hear from you I'll assume you're fine.'

That's all the aftercare I ever give! For greater details of my therapy approach in general – see 'Powerful hypnosis'.

In closing.

No book will cover ALL the things that can come up in a therapy session – you are going to have to add your brains, knowledge, research, initiative, adaptability, people skills and personality (the most important factor) to the mix: I know however that the tools within your deprogramming book will assist you and your clients greatly. Again: I have done it – you can too.

I forgot to mention, there is *one* side effect of reading this book: you might just 'cure' lots of people of addictions! I can live with that. You now have, pretty much, my entire addiction bashing system. Do good with it.

May I finally just say a BIG thank you to all the readers who have left kind words about my books globally on Amazon and Goodreads; I greatly appreciate the time you take in doing do so – in fact I am indebted to you: you have literally changed my life! You take care now! ;) Later babe!

R.H. February 2015.

23726093R00184

Printed in Great Britain
by Amazon